D1083434

TOTALITARIANISM IN PERSPECTIVE

Totalitarianism in Perspective: Three Views

CARL J. FRIEDRICH
MICHAEL CURTIS
BENJAMIN R. BARBER

PRAEGER PUBLISHERS

New York • Washington • London

PRAEGER PUBLISHERS
111 Fourth Avenue, New York, N.Y. 10003, U.S.A.
5, Cromwell Place, London S.W.7, England

Published in the United States of America in 1969
by Praeger Publishers, Inc.

Library of Congress Catalog Card Number: 78-76787

Printed in the United States of America

Contents

Preface

The dialogue here presented on the future of totalitarianism has grown out of a panel held at Chicago as part of the APSA convention of 1967. My original paper has been considerably expanded and altered in light of the comment then made. Since Herb Spiro, one of the commentators, spent the year 1967-68 abroad, his associate in commenting on my paper on that occasion, Ben Barber, agreed to develop his own particular notions into a new and separate paper, and Michael Curtis chose to elaborate what had been comments into an independent study. There have been some interesting further comments by others since the original panel was held.[1] The occupation of Czechoslovakia in 1968 has contributed a new dimension to the issues here under discussion, although it is difficult at this writing to speak with any assurance of the full implications of this decision of the Soviet Union and its associates to intervene by force in the internal evolution of a Communist state in which no appreciable group of people had requested any such intervention. Had the revolutionary developments which were under way in that country been allowed to go forward, they would have provided the novel process of a Communist party consciously and deliberately abandoning a totalitarian for a nontotalitarian regime. Evidently this sort of reversal was too much for the rulers of the Kremlin to witness—whether out of fear of its spreading is still hotly contested among specialists—and hence they labeled it a "counterrevolution" and mounted an effort at suppressing it by force of arms.[2] Just what the implications of it for the theory and practice of totalitarianism are remain to be seen.

No doubt the debate over totalitarianism and the regimes shaped by it will continue for some time to come. It is nonetheless our hope that this rather frank debate over the merits of the term and the reality to which it refers will help those who may wish to employ it in the years to come. It is at times asserted that the new lines which have been developed in the field of comparative government and politics since the early 1950's, especially in the United States, make the notion of a totalitarian regime anachronistic.[3] Whether this will prove to be the case will to some extent depend upon how permanent these new lines prove themselves to be. In any case, the three of us are reasonably aware of these trends and have made allowance for them to the extent our assessment of their truth-value seemed to call for it. To keep hold of what Kenneth Galbraith has mockingly labeled "conventional wisdom" is as important in political theory as it is in practice. The political scientist must seek a middle road between excessive traditionalism and heedless novelty-seeking. In such an effort, the three of us come out at different points, and that does to some extent explain the differences in our conclusions.

My paper, which provided the original challenge, has been placed at the end, partly because my name is the third in an alphabetical order, but also because an earlier version, namely that presented at Chicago, has since been published,[4] and this new one is in some respects a reply to my critics as well. Logically, too, Barber's primarily conceptual exploration can claim the opening position. It is the first comprehensive review of the literature, though Spiro's article in the *International Encyclopedia of the Social Sciences* should also be mentioned in this connection. Rather extensive exploration of the Continental and, more particularly, German writings is found in the magistral cooperative volume by Dietrich Bracher and Associates.[5]

We do not report in these papers any significant advance in causal explanation of the totalitarian phenomenon. It is increasingly clear, however, that there is no *one* single cause, but a considerable variety of explanations, ranging from the strictly personal one as couched in terms of the personality of a Stalin or a Hitler to the broadly sociological and historical ones such as Hannah Arendt's argument about imperialism as the seedbed of the totalitarian systems that have arisen in this century. I have stressed from the beginning that neither communism nor fascism was ideologically conceived in totalitarian terms, but both developed as such as they struggled to put into practice what the realization of a totalist ideology demanded.[6] That such an ideology typically implied a utopian goal has often been observed. The difficulty with this assertion arises from Marx's use of the term "utopian" as a pejorative term by which to describe the earlier socialist writings, especially when involving anarchist aspects. It is often forgotten that the "utopianism" Marx had in mind in criticizing these writers was not primarily what they envisaged as the future society, but rather their failure to appreciate the necessity of a class struggle for overthrowing the established capitalist order.[7] Surely such a goal as the withering away of the state has proved thoroughly utopian in the course of the history of the Soviet Union and other

Communist states. Hence, one is justified in saying that the unattainability of the goal the totalist ideology envisages leads to an extreme straining of the power resources of the leadership engaged in such an enterprise. Modern technology, furthermore, has placed at the disposal of power holders techniques which possess a totalitarian potential.

World War I probably played a fairly important role in initiating some of these techniques, since it taxed the resources of the rival powers to the utmost.[8] I concluded a brief study of this aspect with the statement that "the First World War appears to be a link in the chain of 'causes' which constitute the history of the rise of totalitarian dictatorship." It set the stage for the rise of totalitarian dictatorship, so to speak. The emotional and esthetic implications of this "total war" are evident in a number of literary works; they highlighted such catch-phrases as that of the *Materialschlacht*, literally the battle of materials (rather than human beings).[9] These complex relations have been explored in a number of works discussed below, notably Rothe, Nolte and others. These works, and many others concerned with the rise of fascism and National Socialism as well as Sovietism have contributed to a more differentiated understanding of the enormous complexity of any causal explanation of the phenomenon of totalitarianism. They have tended to reinforce the impression that totalitarian regimes constitute a relatively novel species in the long history of autocratic government.[10]

The dialogue here presented does not pretend to be the decisive, let alone the final, word in the ongoing discussion on totalitarianism. The term is likely to stay with us in political argumentation for quite a few years, exasperating in its iridescent multiplicity of meanings and associations—a quality it shares with many other political key terms, for example, democracy. And, since some of its referents are among the most challenging political phenomena of our time, it will be difficult to discard the term in political studies. Hence the urgency of clarifying its possible meanings for scientific discourse. It is hoped that the pages which follow will offer a contribution, even though not a definitive one.

CARL J. FRIEDRICH
Cambridge, Massachusetts

NOTES

1. Cf. Robert Burrowes, "Totalitarianism—The Revised Standard Version" in *World Politics*, January, 1969, pp. 272-94, where others are referred to a review article of the second editions of the works by Arendt and myself. The English version of Hans Buchheim's study under the title of *Totalitarian Rule: Its Nature and Characteristics* (Middletown, Conn.: Wesleyan University Press, 1968), should be mentioned here. A number of collections of writings (selected) have brought together divergent viewpoints, notably Betty B. Burch, *Dictatorship and Totalitarianism* (Princeton, N.J.: Van Nostrand, 1964), and Paul T. Mason, *Totalitarianism—Temporary Madness or Permanent Danger?* (Boston: D. C. Heath, 1967). The latter raises explicitly what is also at the core of this debate.

2. *Problems of Communism*, XVII, No. 3 (May-June, 1968) 32 ff.

3. Burrowes, *loc. cit.*, p. 289, where he writes "the original editions of both volumes have the added misfortune of having been written just prior to a time when the conduct of inquiry in comparative and empirical political theory was taking a distinctively new turn." Whether this was a misfortune or rather the opposite remains to be seen.

4. In *Problems of Communism, op. cit.*

5. Dietrich Bracher, Wolfgang Sauer, and Gerhard Schulz, *Die national-sozialistische Machtergreifung*, 1960, esp. pp. 3 ff. (Bracher), 371 ff. (Schulz), and 806 ff. (Sauer).

6. Cf. what is said on "totalism" in Ben Barber's paper. Cf. also R. J. Lifton, *Thought Reform and the Psychology of Totalism: A Study of Brainwashing in China* (New York: W. W. Norton, 1961), and C. J. Friedrich and Z. K. Brzezinski, *Totalitarian Dictatorship and Autocracy*, Rev. ed. (New York: Frederick A. Praeger, 1967), pp. 16 ff.

7. "It was this choice of method [namely to persuade those in power] which was natural enough under the circumstances, that has led to the classification of St. Simon, Fourier, and Owen as Utopian socialists." p. 102, Paul M. Sweezey, *Socialism*, 1949. Cf. also the statement by Lenin, cited in Alfred G. Meyer, *Leninism* (New York: Frederick A. Praeger, 1957), p. 189: "What constitutes the utopian character of the plans of the old advocates of cooperation, beginning with Robert Owen? It is the fact that they dreamed of a peaceful transformation of contemporary society to socialism, without taking into account such basic questions as the class war, the conquest of political power by the working class, and the overthrow of the rule of the class exploiters." This is a quote from Lenin "On Cooperation" in *Selected Works*, Vol. IX, p. 408.

8. Cf. my paper "The Rise of Totalitarian Dictatorship" in *World War I: A Turning Point in Modern History* (New York: Alfred A. Knopf, 1967), edited with Introduction and Conclusion by Jack J. Roth who, in his conclusion (p. 132), speaks of the "totalitarianism of the thirties" as one of the sequels that were "if not war-dominated" then at least "war-related." It had its "roots" in World War I. The "totalist" implications of total war are the key point.

9. On Ernst Juenger, cf. Klausfrieder Bastian, *Das Politische bei Ernst Juenger* (Heidelberg [Diss.], 1963); also Hans-Peter Schwarz, *Der Konservative Anarchist: Politik und Zeitkritik Ernst Juenger* (Freiburg, 1962). Cf. also for this literary aspect of the totalitarian syndrome Wolfgang Rothe, *Schriftsteller und totalitaere Welt*, 1966, and Ernst Nolte, *Three Faces of Fascism* (New York: Holt, Rinehart & Winston, 1966). (Original, 1963.)

10. Cf., e.g., Elizabeth Wiskemann, *Europe of the Dictators, 1919-1945* (New York: Harper & Row, 1966). Another interesting attempt to locate totalitarian regimes in the history of government is Eleonore Sterling's *Der Unvollkommene Staat—Studien ueber Diktatur und Demokratie*, 1965; the last three chapters, VI-VIII, are devoted to totalitarian dictatorship.

TOTALITARIANISM IN PERSPECTIVE

1.

Conceptual Foundations
of Totalitarianism

BENJAMIN R. BARBER

A quarter of a century ago Sigmund Neumann, in propounding the need for a new concept to deal with the unique perversities of modern dictatorship, warned that

> ... a continuous misinterpretation of basic concepts is visible and extremely dangerous within the fast-moving social and political sciences which are especially affected by the time lag between ideological perception and historical reality. A heritage of a quarter of a century's standing is often used. In a time of transition such a situation may be deadly.[1]

The term Neumann adopted for his incisive examination of the new dictatorships of the 1920's and 1930's was totalitarianism. In the twenty-five years that have elapsed since his *Permanent Revolution* first appeared, this political construct has become one of the most fashionable and widely employed ideas in comparative political analysis. As a major instrument in the study of communist regimes, and as a more general category for comparison and classification of political systems, its place in the vocabulary of contemporary social science seems secure. Security

3

in the world of political concepts may, however, be "deadly" precisely in the sense anticipated by Neumann. The realities the term was originally introduced to describe have been metamorphosized by time: The regimes of the right, whose appearance the theory of totalitarianism was meant to explain, have been vanquished to the realm of historical controversy; those of the left, which have more recently been brought into the totalitarian conceptual orbit, have undergone fundamental (if unexpected) changes and have been joined by apparently novel species of the postulated genus. Yet both the concept of totalitarianism and the ideological perspective out of which it grew linger on—despite increasing dissatisfaction among many students of comparative politics with its definitional ambiguities and despite an almost complete absence of consensus on the specific regimes to which the term can be appropriately applied.

On the whole, the effort has been to use rather than to understand the concept; unlike such comparable ideas as democracy and dictatorship, totalitarianism has only infrequently been subjected to systematic conceptual analysis in the context of political theory and comparative method.[2] This may be due in some part to the traumatic conditions in which the concept first appeared; like Neumann's pioneering study, most subsequent discussions of totalitarianism have taken the form of empirical studies of concrete political systems generally regarded as unfriendly to the United States. The mood of political crisis and ideological urgency that surrounded such studies naturally gave to totalitarianism a controversial, sometimes polemical aura from which the term has never been satisfactorily emancipated.[3] Where one theorist perceives in totalitarianism only an inappropriately pejorative antonym for laissez-faire,[4] another speaks darkly of the "absolute evil" that accompanies the "final stages of its evolution."[5] Still a third, essaying to utilize the concept in a theory of development, complains that it "has been applied so loosely as to become virtually meaningless in communicating any specific meaning."[6]

The vagaries in definition and usage suggested by these disagreements point, in my view, not only to the probability that reality has outgrown the concept, but also to the possibility of fundamental inadequacies in the concept itself—inadequacies that have been present from the outset. It will be argued in what follows that the vision of political reality upon which the idea of totalitarianism is founded not only is unreflective of modern political experience, but was antiquated at the time the idea was first employed. The emphasis will be not on the disparities between the implications of the totalitarian construct and the political realities to which it has been applied (disparities that have been provocatively explored in this volume by Michael Curtis and elsewhere by Herbert J. Spiro and others[7]), but on the prerequisites and the implications of the concept itself in terms of its place in the language of comparative politics and its adequacy as an organizing and classifying construct for both historical and contemporary regimes and ideas. Hopefully, this emphasis will reveal not only the inadequacies of the totalitarian construct, but the barrenness of the assumptions about political life that underlie it.

Because this task is explicative rather than stipulative, it seems prudent to commence with a brief review of the manner(s) in which totalitarianism has been used. Unfortunately, explicating definitions can often be more troublesome than inventing them (which may explain the penchant of political analysts for ignoring prior formulations set forth by their colleagues in favor of their own renderings of the concept), especially when disagreement

extends beyond the concept itself to the ground rules that
guide usage. In its adjectival form, totalitarianism often
seems to have become little more than a vague if caustic
pejorative, which has been good-naturedly appropriated by
word-starved critics in unrelated disciplines. Where most
political scientists would have been content with the
physical terrors of political totalitarianism, one literary
critic has permitted his perfervid imagination to conjure up
the nightmarish possibilities of a "totalitarian" syntax.[8]
But even when we restrict ourselves to social science
usage—we can, after all, hardly be held responsible for
the whims of literary phrase-makers—totalitarianism has
been used in conjunction not only with specified political
systems, but also with "movements,"[9] "parties,"[10] "leaders,"[11] "processes,"[12] and "ideas"[13] in a manner that,
aside from its exclamatory overtones, makes it impossible
to determine whether the modifier "totalitarian" connotes
membership as a subset, on the part of the noun modified,
in the category "totalitarian regime" or refers simply to
individual characteristics of the noun modified irrespective
of its relationship to totalitarian (or nontotalitarian)
regimes; does "totalitarian party" denote any party operating within a totalitarian regime or a party with particular
attributes operating anywhere? In the latter case, nontotalitarian parties are theoretically conceivable within totalitarian regimes, and totalitarian parties are possible in
nontotalitarian regimes;[14] in the former case, these possibilities are by definition excluded. As if these semantic
uncertainties did not provide sufficient confusion, exponents of the concept—often at odds with one another
—have insisted on the appropriateness of the concept
totalitarianism to a menagerie of political systems whose
range and scope would astonish the most catholic and
undiscriminating of political analysts. Among the regimes
(real and utopian) that have been labeled totalitarian are to
be found not only apparent prototypes like the Soviet

Union,[15] Nazi Germany,[16] and fascist Italy,[17] but also Russia in its "Caesero-papist" period under the Czars,[18] traditional India during the period of the Mauryu dynasty,[19] the Roman Empire in the reign of Diocletian,[20] Plato's ideal republic,[21] China—not only in its current Communist phase[22] but in the period of the Ch'in Dynasty,[23] the United States in the 1960's[24] and in the 1840's,[25] certain versions of the medieval Christian Commonwealth,[26] the ancient polis of Sparta,[27] a variety of modern developing regimes,[28] Hobbes's Leviathan,[29] Meiji Japan,[30] Geneva under Calvin,[31] and certain varieties of European feudalism.[32]

This compilation, however, does not in itself warrant dismissal of the concept that serves as its common denominator, for the suspicion persists that there may be a tenuous strand of identity running through this otherwise outlandishly disparate catalog of political systems. And the focus here is, in any case, meant to be the concept itself and not the systems to which it has rightly or wrongly been applied. Moving then from the character of the object (the systems to which totalitarianism has been applied) to the nature of the subject (the character of totalitarianism itself, in abstract terms), a rather different compilation can be made.

Elsewhere in this volume, Carl J. Friedrich tenders a restatement of what has become a seminal definition:

> The features which distinguish [totalitarian] regimes from other and older autocracies, as well as from Western-type democracies, are six in number: (1) a totalist ideology; (2) a single party committed to this ideology and usually led by one man, the dictator; (3) a fully developed secret police; and three kinds of monopoly or, more precisely, monopolistic control: namely that of (a) mass communications; (b) operational weapons; (c) all organizations, including economic ones.[33]

There are, however, a multiplicity of alternative and often contradictory definitions competing with Friedrich's classic formulation. The list that follows then, although not exhaustive, is representative of the range of language which has been employed in delimiting and identifying the concept of totalitarianism. In this spirit, the definitions given below have been selected to illustrate a spectrum of possibilities rather than to reflect precisely and accurately the position of the writers cited. This is to some extent making a virtue of necessity, for the texts from which the compilation has been culled are, for the most part, not particularly susceptible to succinct epigrammatic exegesis. Indeed, many of the concept's most spirited exponents fail to give the slightest conceptual clue about construction and usage, apparently content to leave it to the more serious among their readers to divine what is "really" meant by the term.[34]

With these caveats in mind, and remembering too that the more exotic and garish formulae have been intentionally omitted from the list,[35] the reader is asked to peruse the following definitions,[36] presented in alphabetical order by author:

Total terror destroys the space between [men] . . .[37] total terror [is] the essence of totalitarianism.

(Hannah Arendt)

Totalitarianism [is] . . . a new form of government falling into the general classification of dictatorship . . . a system in which technologically advanced instruments of political power are wielded without restraint by centralized leadership of an elite movement, for the purpose of effecting a total social revolution, including the conditioning of man on the basis of certain arbitrary ideological assumptions proclaimed by the leadership, in an atmosphere of coerced unanimity of the entire population.[38]

(Zbigniew K. Brzezinski)

Is there a "totalitarianism" in the abstract, or as an ideal type . . . or are there only particular totalitarian systems? [It may be] answered tentatively that there are particular totalitarian systems which are comparable among each other to the extent to which they have certain limited performance characteristics in common. The three most important of these characteristics are perhaps extreme mobilization of effort, unity of command, and effective power of enforcement.[39]

(Karl Deutsch)

The essence of totalitarianism, then, is that it annihilates all boundaries between the state and the groupings of society, even the state and the individual personality.[40]

(Harry Eckstein and David E. Apter)

The danger of totalitarianism [is] raised by the policy of economic planning.[41]

(Frederick Hayek)

We define [totalitarianism] merely as a set of methods used, under certain circumstances, by a group or several groups in control of a government in order to retain that control.[42]

(John H. Kautsky)

The basic conception of centralized totalitarianism, as well as its most important instruments, arose prior to industrialism and independently of industrialism.

. . .

In pre-industrial societies, as in modern times, the purpose of [totalitarian] centralized political controls is to coordinate as far as possible the activities of a society in the pursuit of a single goal.[43]

(Barrington Moore, Jr.)

What distinguishes [totalitarianism] from absolutism is not primarily the caesaristic element . . . but rather the destruction of the line between state and society and the total politicization of society by the device of the monopolistic party.[44]

(Franz Neumann)

The total state of today above all implies continuous dynamics which cannot be stopped unless stopped permanently. The first aim of totalitarianism is to perpetuate and to institutionalize revolution.[45]

(Sigmund Neumann)

What we call nowadays totalitarianism belongs to a tradition which is just as old or just as young as our civilization itself . . . [the tradition of] Utopian social engineering . . . historicism . . . and the closed society.[46]

(Karl Popper)

> The totalitarian democratic school . . . is based upon the assumption of a sole and exclusive truth in politics. It may be called political Messianism in the sense that it postulates a preordained, harmonious and perfect scheme of things, to which men are irresistibly driven, and at which they are bound to arrive. It recognizes ultimately only one plane of existence, the political. It widens the scope of politics to embrace the whole of human existence . . . it is vital to add that much of the totalitarian democratic attitude was contained in the . . . eighteenth-century pattern of thought.[47]
>
> (J. L. Talmon)

The most cursory perusal of this extraordinary compilation reveals contrasts in definition as fundamental and striking as those in application evidenced by the list of regimes noted above. Before attempting to extract from such diversified definitions a shared emphasis, it may be useful to treat systematically the elements that distinguish these multiple constructions of totalitarianism from one another; the definitions may be classified according to at least three major distinctions, as well as a number of secondary ones that seem at least indirectly related to them. Many disputes about the nature of totalitarianism or about the applicability of the concept to particular regimes can be traced to confusion about or neglect of these distinctions.

A primary distinction can be made between what might be called phenomenological and essentialist uses of the term totalitarianism. Phenomenological definitions of totalitarianism "attempt to isolate its objective attributes";[48] that is to say, they identify the concept with a " 'syndrome' or pattern of interrelated traits,"[49] or with "certain limited performance characteristics"[50] that describe the objective (and thus measurable) behavioral and institutional characteristics of a particular class of regimes. Such definitions generally eschew, or at least minimize, questions of ideology (especially ideological content) and ends, and are usually concrete rather than abstract. Of the above formulations, those of John Kautsky and Karl Deutsch appear most phenomenological, followed by that of Carl Friedrich. The descriptive potential of phenomenological definitions has apparently not been overlooked by social scientists recently engaged in quantitatively oriented cross-polity survey research. Both in the Banks and Textor survey[51] and in R. J. Rummel's current project, totalitarianism is employed without qualification as a primary-factor dimension; in the Rummel study, it is used in a typically phenomenological manner to label a factor whose indicators comprise "freedom of opposition, voting system and press censorship."[52]

Essentialist, or what some prefer to call "real,"[53] definitions include not simply those that, like Arendt's, take the form "the essence of totalitarianism is . . . " but all formulations that emphasize ideological content, system goals, and other relatively abstract and nonmeasurable attributes of a regime. Although "planning" is, in itself, susceptible to objectification and measurement, the way in which it is treated by Hayek indicates an essentialist preoccupation—as does Popper's confrontation with "historicism" and "Utopian social engineering" or Arendt's apocalyptic vision of "total terror" and the "radical evil" into which it is ultimately transformed. The definitions given by Sigmund Neumann, Talmon, and Brzezinski are also informed with an essentialist bias, albeit they—along with several marginally essentialist definitions (for example, Moore and Franz Neumann)—are not exclusively essentialist in that they often provide a set of performance characteristics as concrete, if weak, indicators for the abstract attributes they posit. Thus, Brzezinski is willing to incorporate a set of "objective attributes," like the one suggested by Friedrich, into the definition of totalitarianism, but, ultimately, his definition "goes beyond Friedrich's descriptive syndrome . . . and attempts to point also to its essence—i.e., its institutionalized revolutionary zeal."[54]

Both the phenomenological and the essentialist approaches have serious methodological limitations. Phenomenological definitions of totalitarianism, although they provide unequivocal criteria for the classification of regimes on the basis of measurable indicators, tend toward an ambiguous catholicity when actually applied. Strictly speaking, there are few elements in the totalitarian syndrome as depicted by Deutsch, Eckstein and Apter, or, even, Friedrich that cannot, to some degree, be found in all modern, developed political systems: "totalitarianism is an artifact of modern life. . . . The plain fact is that most of the requisites of mass democracy are also requisites of totalitarianism: widely diffused education . . . a highly developed technology . . . a mobile society, rational modes of conduct, sufficient leisure for political participation, and considerable organizational skill."[55] Totalitarianism, phenomenologically conceived, thus lends inadvertent support to theories holding that all fully developed industrial regimes are "converging" in their significant political and economic essentials. Whether such theories are used to demonstrate that all centralized industrial bureaucracies are becoming increasingly totalitarian,[56] or to show that concepts like totalitarianism are becoming increasingly irrelevant to the common economic, cultural, and psychological dilemmas of the "have" nations (as against those of the "have nots"),[57] they render totalitarianism as a concept incapable of meaningful analytic discrimination.

Essentialist definitions are a good deal more secure from appropriation by exponents of convergence, but they achieve this security only by virtue of their semantic imprecision, their theoretical elusiveness, and their ideological emotivism[58]—methodological shortcomings far more nefarious than those that plague phenomenologists. What Leo Strauss has written about the term "authoritarian" suits remarkably well the essentialist approach to totalitarianism: "When social scientists distinguish between democratic and authoritarian [read "totalitarian"] habits or types of human beings, what they call 'authoritarian' is in all cases known to me a caricature of everything of which they, as democrats of a certain kind, disapprove."[59] It is generally accepted that political science has no room for analytic concepts that pretend to define objective characteristics of observed phenomena when they are, in actuality, defining only the ideological attitudes of the observer. Yet of the definitions given above, none are entirely "objective" and several—to a degree that would probably correlate well with their essentialism—appear to be almost entirely polemical in nature.

Neither usage, then, appears to be free of serious methodological pitfalls. Moreover, these initial difficulties are compounded and multiplied by a number of related secondary distinctions in usage. Implicit already in the initial distinction between essentialist and phenomenological approaches is an "analytic objectivity" criterion according to which the set of general definitions can be classified into emotive and nonemotive subsets; however, because emotivism appears to some degree to define (analytically) essentialism, setting up this criterion as an independent factor is, if not analytically redundant, at least unnecessary.

But another distinction—this one logically independent but nonetheless related—can be made between various definitions according to the relative simplicity or complexity of the explanatory model utilized. Essentialist definitions tend to rely somewhat more on monocausal analysis (or, if one wishes to avoid the implications of causality, single-factor analysis), while phenomenological definitions, by virtue of their syndromic character, are generally multicausal. The idea of "essence" is, after all, singular rather than plural. Of course, phenomenological definitions may emphasize certain individual factors as being more "decisive" than others, and essentialist definitions may (as in Brzezinski) incorporate, in addition to a single paramount focus, several secondary factors. Nonetheless, the distinction persists, making the reconciliation of competing formulations yet more complicated.

Another distinction can be drawn between definitions that, in content or in emphasis, are rigorously political and those that focus on economic and social determinants. For Franz Neumann, totalitarianism is a form of dictatorship and, hence, a pre-eminently political entity.[60] Eckstein and Apter, on the other hand, "prefer to talk about totalitarian societies rather than totalitarian governments or totalitarian states."[61] For Hayek, the term denotes only a general approach to economic organization. Distinctions of this kind tend to mislead and confuse, not only in that they raise the unhappy possibility of one term being applied to what in reality are completely discrete processes, but also in that they cut across, and thus complicate, our previous distinctions. Both Sigmund Neumann, who is inclined to essentialist usage, and Karl Deutsch, whose definition represents a phenomenological paradigm, appear to understand totalitarianism in primarily political terms—although their conceptions of politics probably differ significantly.

The distinction between political and extrapolitical definitions points to still another question over which advocates of the totalitarian construct have been deeply divided: Is totalitarianism *sui generis*, a qualitatively unique form of political (or socio-economic) organization, or does it represent a determinate set of quantitatively variable attributes that, although when taken separately and in moderation may characterize a variety of regimes, become, when intensified and combined, politically noxious and, thus, "totalitarian"? The first view suggests that regimes either are or are not totalitarian and that totalitarianism is a qualitatively distinctive political form analytically discrete from, and thus not capable of being subsumed under such logically comparable forms as, tyranny, authoritarianism, or dictatorship. The latter view implies that systems may be more or less totalitarian depending upon the number, intensity, and syndromic interdependence of attributes present and thus suggests that totalitarianism is a quantitatively measurable species of some broader genus, such as dictatorship or autocracy (or even, as Talmon asserts, democracy). The notion that totalitarianism is a question of degree rather than of kind is often associated with multicausal explanations whose syndromic character permits meaningful quantitative differentiation; single-factor explanations, on the other hand, because they are simplistic and exclusive, lend themselves to the thesis that totalitarianism is unique. Because monocausal definitions are usually essentialist, it would in turn appear that essentialist arguments postulate uniqueness. In fact, this is not always the case—not because such relationships are theoretically unsound but because most definitions of totalitarianism do not rest on sound theory. Franz Neumann, despite his proclivity for essentialism, treats the concept as a subset of dictatorship.[62] Carl Friedrich, although phenomenologically oriented, nonetheless insists on totalitarianism's uniqueness, if only as a novel genus of the traditional species "autocracy."[63]

The real importance of this particular secondary distinction lies, however, not in the light it sheds on the self-contradictory character of several definitions but in the clue it provides for a second primary distinction (like the one separating phenomenological and essentialist arguments) that pervades the discussion of totalitarianism, a distinction that separates "modernist" interpretations, which understand totalitarianism as a "historical innovation" made possible only recently by "the technological state of modern society,"[64] from "traditionalist" interpretations, which perceive in it a political condition "as young or old as civilization itself."[65] The critical question here turns on the problem of the historical stability of political classifications. Can systems of collective life (political, economic, and social) be accounted for by universal logical distinctions applied indifferently over time, or are separate and evolving categories of analysis required for the changing conditions of successive eras? The citation from Neumann with which this essay began clearly favors a conceptual relativism and, in fact, a majority of definitions link totalitarianism with purportedly unique characteristics of modern life (a sophisticated technology, rational bureaucracy, mass production and mass media, industrialism, and so forth). However, it would be a mistake to conclude from this, as Robert Tucker and others apparently have, that totalitarianism has been conceived exclusively "as a distinctively new, twentieth-century development in the theory and practice of despotism."[66] A number of theorists find the modernist claim to be "highly dubious,"[67] and contend that "the basic conception of centralized totalitarianism, as well as its most important instruments, arose prior to industrialism and independently of industrialism."[68] Traditionalist arguments quite naturally stress the political element in totalitarianism, for economic and social factors have indisputably undergone radical transformation in the last century and to give these traits prominence would be tantamount to abandoning traditionalism by default.

A certain pattern begins to reveal itself: Traditionalist definitions are generally political; political definitions focus on single factors; single-factor analysis tends to be essentialist. Karl Popper's definition—traditionalist, highly political, monocausal, and strongly essentialist—emerges as a paradigm at one end of the logical spectrum; Carl

Friedrich's—modernist, emphasizing political variables that are dependent on economic and social structure, multi-causal, and relatively phenomenological—presents itself as the dichotomous parameter. Unfortunately, this engaging theoretical symmetry—although paradigmatic—is only infrequently approximated in most definitions, which appear to be preoccupied more with their appositeness to specific regimes than with their internal coherence. Several modernist definitions (for example, Sigmund Neumann's and Karl Deutsch's) are nonetheless rigorously political, which brings both their modernism and their "politicity" under suspicion.

Peculiarly enough, in addition to their theoretical incoherence, traditionalist definitions raise a dilemma not unsimilar to the one that confronts phenomenological interpretations. Phenomenologists, as we have seen, in excluding dictatorships of the *ancien regime* from the totalitarian category in order to demonstrate the dependence of totalitarianism on a syndrome of unprecedented economic and social developments, are inadvertently forced to a typological catholicity that brings almost all fully industrialized states at least partially into the totalitarian orbit. In the same manner, essentialist-oriented traditionalists, in denying the dependence on the modern syndrome of what they understand as totalitarianism, are led to a historical catholicity that encompasses as totalitarian a multitude of centralist regimes ranging back through history to man's earliest political experience.

To construe totalitarianism either way is to create a gargantuan and unwieldy framework for political classification, a framework that brings into a single set the most disparate and unlikely political regimes—for example, the United States, Nazi Germany, and the Soviet Union on the one hand, the Han dynasty, Plato's Republic, and Calvinist Geneva on the other. In neither case are we provided with an instrument capable of very much analytic discrimina-

tion; in neither case do the criteria of significance that
must underlie all distinctions in comparative politics seem
very convincing.[69]

There is still another major question that divides those
who employ the concept of totalitarianism: the question
of whether democracy is logically antithetical to it or, in
some form, compatible with it. Putting aside possible
empirical relationships, it would appear at first glance that
the two are—despite their respective definitional ambiguities—logically antithetical. Many students of politics would
concur with Bertram Wolfe in perceiving in totalitarianism
and democracy "rival twentieth-century philosoph[ies] of
government, with corresponding governmental structure[s],"[70] but more than a few take seriously an
alternative view that Wolfe dismisses (with unwarranted
glibness) as "conservative." In this view, democracy can be
"a breeding ground for totalitarianism,"[71] both "totalitarian Messianic" and "empirical and liberal."[72] This position
is rooted in a peculiar kind of conceptual bigamy, which
weds totalitarianism, in one of its guises, to a "historic,
racial and organic" philosophy of the right, and, in a
different guise, to an "essentially individualistic, atomistic
and rational" philosophy of the left (that is, democracy).[73]
It also points to the liberal roots of the totalitarian thesis
(examined below) in that it represents a latter-day version
of the traditional liberal critique of mass democracy found
in the writings of, among others, de Tocqueville,[74] Lord
Acton, or Ortega y Gassett who, in the following excerpt,
seems to anticipate totalitarianism understood as democracy: "Today we are witnessing the triumph of a
hyperdemocracy in which the mass acts directly, outside
the law, imposing its aspirations and its desires."[75]

The adoption by modern social scientists of traditional
liberal beliefs holding that "democracy, wielding its power
as a whole, can overwhelm the individual with its
tyranny . . . can engulf liberalism and sweep freedoms

away . . . "[76] (exemplified by the concept of "totalitarian democracy") also finds a reflection in the current socio-psychological preoccupation with the pernicious influence on liberal individualism exercised by mass society,[77] mass movements,[78] and mass man as the alienated and impotent (subjectively incompetent) by-product of modern industrial society.[79] It is sometimes justified by an empirical appeal to "the plain fact . . . that most of the requisites of mass democracy are also requisites of totalitarianism."[80]

Unfortunately, the dispute over whether totalitarian systems are compatible with certain varieties of, or elements in, democracy cuts across the lines separating essentialists from phenomenologists (Talmon and Popper, for example, though both essentialists, take contradictory positions), as well as those dividing traditionalists from modernists (although on opposite sides of the question of totalitarianism's novelty, both Friedrich and Moore take it to be antithetical to Western democracy). This third major issue appears, then, only to cast further conceptual gloom over a subject in urgent need of illumination. Indeed, the major conclusion to be drawn from this rather elaborate, but by no means exhaustive, account of the scope and interdependence of discrepancies in usage and ambiguities in definition that surround the term is that totalitarianism is to modern political science what reason was to Luther: a conceptual harlot of uncertain parentage, belonging to no one but at the service of all.

This conclusion does, however, require serious modification. As we suggested before setting out to explore discrepancies in usage and definition, there is to be found in all interpretations, however dissimilar, a shared emphasis and a common focus that point to a set of underlying assumptions about politics upon which almost all advocates of the concept of totalitarianism seem to agree. It is to the character of this common focus and to the nature of the political premises upon which the commonality rests that we must now turn attention. Hopefully, in the course of the examination that follows, some of the problems in definition raised above can be resolved.

In order to depict accurately the unifying element in different definitions of totalitarianism, it is useful to withdraw to a distance where it becomes possible to examine the general perspective of political analysis within which totalitarianism functions as a concept. In necessarily rudimentary terms, the study of politics can be circumscribed by at least three interconnected but logically distinct political questions: in traditional language, the question of rulership (who governs?), the question of ends (to what end?), and the question of scope (within what sphere?); or, in the language of systems theory, the question of inputs (rulership treated in terms of process rather than institutions, in terms, that is, of political socialization and recruitment, and interest aggregation and articulation), the question of outputs (procedural and substantive norms governing the processes of making, interpreting, and executing law), and the question of system boundaries (which define functionally, and thus delimit, the system). Almost all of the strictly political issues that concern modern political scientists can be defined and treated in the framework of these three questions. Legitimacy, for example, can be understood as a function of the democratic or popular form of rulership (guaranteeing consensus on system rules), the pluralistic position on ends (guaranteeing the possibility of change from below), and the constitutional or limited government (*laissez-faire*) approach to the question of scope (since minimizing the pale of government activity tends to maximize the spheres of private life in which the question of legitimacy does not arise), or as a function of some other combination of answers to our three fundamental questions.

The task of a systematic political vocabulary is to identify and discriminate between the different processes associated with alternative answers to fundamental questions such as the ones posited above. The Greeks, for example, were careful to distinguish between the problem of rulership and that of just or lawful rule; it was not enough to answer the question "who rules?" without satisfying the query "in whose interest?" The traditional trilogy of monarchy, aristocracy, and democracy was expanded to include the perverted forms of tyranny, oligarchy, and mob rule, thus providing a matrix in which any particular regime could be plotted in two political dimensions simultaneously.[81] Although usage is far more complicated today, vestiges of these ancient distinctions persist. Isaiah Berlin, for example, notes that "there is no necessary connection between individual liberty and democratic rule. The answer to the question 'Who governs me?' is logically distinct from the question 'How far does government interfere with me?' "[82] If "liberalism" is used, then, to denote a form of limited government, and "democracy" to denote popular rulership, then liberalism and democracy are neither compatible nor competitive responses to a single political problem, but logically unrelated answers to two distinct kinds of political questions, though these questions may be empirically related as independent variables.

Using the same logic, it is clear that collectivism, if we define it as a system in which ends are conceived of in monolithic, absolute terms, does not necessarily entail the absence of democracy (in the narrow sense delimited above) or the presence of extensive interference by the state in the "private sphere," but connotes only the existence of a monistic ideology devoted to holistic political objectives. In theory, we can conceive of a democratic, liberal, collectivist state—that is, a regime in which rulership is popular, governmental scope is limited, and objectives are collective—for democracy, liberalism, and collectivism as defined here are related synthetically rather than analytically. This is not to assert that they are unrelated, for the questions to which these three concepts respond, while logically distinct, cannot be, and in fact never are, treated in a political vacuum. Concepts such as these describe from a particular theoretical orientation concrete political and social phenomena that may be empirically correlated (if not causally interdependent). Thus, a central concern of the social sciences becomes the discovery and elucidation of empirical relationships between the logically distinctive kinds of phenomena distinguished by our (or some other) theoretical model.[83]

It is precisely at this point, however, that critical difficulties arise for the concept of totalitarianism as well as for several other constructs or dimension labels employed both by social scientists and by area specialists interested in Communist and Fascist regimes. Too many political scientists, bent on operationalizing terms whose analytic antecedents and logical implications are insufficiently perceived, utilize concepts that covertly presuppose relationships that may, at best, be only probabilistic. "Liberal-democracy" or "constitutional-democracy" are often introduced in a manner that suggests a "natural" relationship when in fact, as we have seen, liberalism and democracy are meaningful only when treated as logically unrelated formulations of different questions—a point that has apparently been better understood by the aristocratic fathers of the American constitution and the *Philosophes* of eighteenth-century France than by contemporary students of comparative politics. The situation deteriorates still further when a single concept is used with reference to several different processes, thus masking the uncertainty of the relationship between them; democracy is often used in a fashion that suggests that popular rule, limited government, and pluralism are different ways of saying the same thing and that "democracy" is the construct upon which they are all analytically dependent (making the three mutually interdependent).

The confusion becomes complete when we remove ourselves one final step from the logical premises (as well as the empirical data) upon which a conceptual vocabulary must rest and review the comparative pejoratives that have appeared as antonyms for already misunderstood concepts like democracy and liberalism. In this setting, many of the definitional ambiguities surrounding totalitarianism can be explained. Terms like authoritarianism, dictatorship, and, especially, totalitarianism have become, in the usage of many of their devotees, vague, quasi-ideological catchalls for regimes that reflect, in answer to one or more of our basic questions, solutions or combinations of solutions of which the "Western World" disapproves. Totalitarianism becomes a limiting parameter for the continuum whose other parametric limit is democracy, but, because the process these two parameters are meant to delimit is generally left indeterminate—indeed, is often a conceptual mask for several unrelated processes—the one concept is as disconcertingly confusing as the other, to which it is contrasted; in fact, being one more step removed from the model that gives it meaning, it is even more so.

The result of this pervasive conceptual confusion is easily seen in the fruitless disputation that has developed over what totalitarianism "really means." Talmon and Popper clash (by implication) over the compatibility of democracy and totalitarianism, when, in fact, both are right, for Talmon means by democracy only a form of rulership in which the masses become enfranchised, whereas Popper apparently has in mind a regime of limited scope with pluralistic objectives. Talmon's democracy *is* compatible (though not identical) with totalitarianism;

Popper's is not. Similarly, the controversy over whether totalitarianism is uniquely modern or "as young or old as civilization itself" vanishes if we realize that most traditionalists assume that totalitarianism is an answer to the question of ends, while modernists perceive in it a solution to the problem of scope. In defining totalitarianism in terms of the "pursuit of a single goal," Barrington Moore, Jr., can justifiably plead that preindustrial societies may incorporate totalitarian elements without contradicting Eckstein and Apter, who insist that totalitarianism is a distinctly modern function of industrial society, for Eckstein and Apter have in mind not the pursuit of a single goal but the "annihilation" of boundaries between state and society, a condition that may be fully realizable only through such instruments of modern society as a well-developed technology and mass communications.[84]

Does this semantic confusion, and the resulting confusion about what totalitarianism really signifies, mean that the search for a common focus is futile? Probably not. Although this shared emphasis may only be implicit and the sharpness of the resulting analytic picture found wanting, almost all definitions do share a concern for the question of scope—the relationship between the public domain (the state) and the private realm (defined in terms of social groups [society] or atomized individuals). This emphasis is inherent in the root of the word totalitarianism: totalism, not in its purely psychological implications,[85] but as an all-encompassing social and political holism that rejects boundaries and, hence, the fragmented public and private spheres that boundaries define. Totalitarianism "widens the scope of politics to embrace the whole of human existence,"[86] and thus entails "the destruction of the line between state and society and total politicization of society."[87] With the destruction of this line comes the annihilation of "all boundaries between the state and the groupings of society, even the state and the individual personality,"[88] as well as the coordination of "all the material and human resources of . . . society, extending even to the private feelings and sentiments of the populace."[89] In sum, totalitarianism, as "a system of rules for realizing totalist intentions"[90] renders "the scope of government . . . unlimited, so that the mutual behavior of the individual is regulated in every possible aspect of human life."[91] Both essentialist and phenomenological definitions share the concern for totalism, although the former tend to emphasize the processes by which the totalist condition is achieved (for example, terror or revolution), while the latter generally depict the condition itself (the absence of boundaries as given by such indicators as a lack of privacy). A totalist preoccupation is also visible in both traditionalist and modernist definitions, although that preoccupation is, at first glance, less evident in the traditionalists whose chief interest appears to lie in problems of ends rather than of scope; however, it is quickly apparent that underlying the emphasis on monolithic (or simply monist) ends in traditionalist definitions of totalitarianism is the assumption that single-end ideologies tend toward, or even entail, the destruction of privacy and rights—entail, that is to say, a totalism of scope. Again, we find that Apter's differences with Barrington Moore, Jr. can be reduced to different notions about what *causes* totalism (technological, centralized societies—even those pursuing pluralist ends—in the one case, modern *or* traditional societies pursuing monolithic ends in the other), rather than to more fundamental cleavages about totalism, which in itself serves as their common denominator. Similarly, both democratic and nondemocratic definitions are rooted in problems of totalism though they may, by virtue of unstated linkages, employ the language of rulership or ends.[92]

If, then, this focus is reflected in most definitions of totalitarianism, why do so many remain opaque and controversial? Why the definitional discrepancies and the controversies in usage? If the problem of scope is critical, why then are so many approaches to totalitarian systems couched in the language of questions about rulership or ends? The answer to these queries has already been suggested in our previous discussion: Most approaches to totalitarianism are rooted in a set of unstated, unfounded, and often unperceived assumptions linking particular solutions to the problem of scope to purportedly corollary answers to questions of rulership and ends. For Talmon, totalitarianism appears to be intimately related to democracy, but only because Talmon presupposes that under some circumstances the extension of popular participation in government entails—either logically, functionally (as a dependent variable, that is, empirically), or in some other indeterminate manner—a circumscription of the private sphere.[93] This presupposition may or may not be demonstrable, but it is hardly self-evident; yet the term totalitarian conceals both the implicit hypothetical correlation and the necessity for theoretical validation or empirical verification.

In a similar vein, Talmon argues that because, as a result of the breakdown of the division between state and society, totalitarianism "recognizes ultimately only one plane of existence," it must necessarily be "based upon the assumption of a sole and exclusive truth in politics."[94] But again, the presupposition that the absence of a clear-cut separation between the state and the individual entails, or is correlated with, a rejection of pluralistic ends remains misleadingly covert and is probably unwarranted. It is not our task here to test empirically the relationship of particular formulae determining the scope of government to alternative forms of rulership and varying theories about the ends of political society, but it may be legitimate to look into the theoretical infrastructure of what we have called the primary focus of totalitarianism—the question of scope—in the hope of illuminating the sources and limitations of the relationships that have been implied, as well as the ultimate validity of the totalitarian construct itself.

An examination of the paradigm generally utilized in exploring the question of scope reveals that totalitarianism, even when restricted to this primary concern, obscures significant distinctions in favor of a simplistic abstract model that bears little relation to political reality. The relationship between the public and the private spheres, with which the question of scope is concerned, can, after all, be viewed not from one but from at least three quite dissimilar perspectives, each of which produces its own particular variety of totalism. Hence, although totalism represents a common focus of our multiple definitions, it turns out, upon examination, to be little more than a generic term for several very different political conditions related only in the broadest way.

The condition with which totalism is usually associated is produced by the expansion of the public sphere at the expense of the private; this condition, which can be considered the "statist" variety of totalism, entails an aggressive extension of perceived restraints on private activity that is likely to be experienced as repressive. Unhappily, many theorists of totalitarianism have assumed that statism *is* totalism itself, rather than one of its several manifestations. Thus, they are led by way of a logical inversion to the conclusion that whenever boundaries are absent (totalism), coercive means must have been employed to annihilate them (statism). The end condition (absence of boundaries) is taken as conclusive proof that statist means (the coercive extension of the public sphere) have been employed. Once this means-ends (or process-condition) confusion is dispelled, however, it becomes clear that the totalist condition can be engendered by means other than repressive statism. A different perspective reveals the possibility that individuals may perceive in the public realm the fulfillment of their private needs and voluntarily make their concerns as private individuals the focus of the public weal. Here, too, an end condition of totalism may obtain, inasmuch as the affairs of the individual have become the affairs of all, the *res publica*, but it is a condition radically different from the (in form identical) condition produced by statism. For in the "communitarian" variety of totalism (as we would like to call it), the enlarged public sphere is viewed as the only meaningful sphere of life in which freedom, fulfillment, and human purpose can be achieved, while the diminutive private sphere (to the extent it exists at all) is viewed as synonymous with a prepolitical, prehuman realm of pure necessity.[95] The Greek *polis* and the Swiss commune exemplify communitarian forms of totalism that, especially in the philosophies of their interpreters (for example, Plato or Rousseau), have come under attack by critics of totalitarianism, who have apparently failed to distinguish between statist and communitarian totalism, and who assume, with the traditional liberal distaste for politics, that "private life and public order will always be at odds."[96] To such a peculiar bias a student of Greek history could reply, with Aristotle, "that the *polis* is prior in the order of nature to the family and the individual . . . [and that] not being self-sufficient when they are isolated, all individuals are so many parts all equally depending on the whole. The man who is isolated—who is unable to share in the benefits of political association, or has no need because he is already self-sufficient—is no part of the *polis*, and must therefore be either a beast or a god . . . if he be without virtue, he is a most unholy and savage being . . . Justice, which is his salvation, belongs to the *polis*."[97] The liberal perspective then provides one view, but surely not the only view, of totalism.

Still a third perspective on totalism is possible, one that involves neither the conscious and repressive extension of the public domain nor the voluntary integration of the private realm into the public. Under certain circumstances, formal (perhaps constitutional) boundaries may erode quite independently of developments in the public or private realms, causing the two spheres to lose gradually their distinctiveness and to mesh imperceptibly into one another.[98] With statism, coercive means are utilized to infringe and, ultimately, usurp the functions of an unwilling private sector, irrespective of such formal obstacles as constitutional or customary checks on public power; in the case of what, for want of a more graphic term, may be described as "involuntary" totalism, public power, without increasing its scope or jeopardizing its legitimacy, seeps by default into a somnolent private sector under conditions of unconscious conformity that obviate the need for—indeed, exclude the possibility of—coercion. In fact, because this kind of seepage may extend the scope of government well beyond its resources, conformity becomes a necessary prerequisite of involuntary (or creeping) totalism. In comparing this third variation on totalism with the statist variant, certain salient differences emerge. Involuntary totalism is, by definition, evolutionary and "natural"; statism, on the other hand, is radical and revolutionary, the conscious contrivance of a party seeking power.[99] Involuntary (or evolutionary) totalism is thus more likely to be legitimate, resting "on the spontaneous support of nearly the total population,"[100] while a statist regime, whatever its *de facto* status, may have difficulty in attracting the inner loyalty of its political subjects. Freedom, under conditions of statism, will generally be viewed as a function of the absence of external restraints (the classic Lockean and Hobbesian picture); in an environment of involuntary totalism, this view, even if prevalent, can only be misleading, for liberty here will necessarily entail resistance to internal psychological restraints and subliminal manipulation, a characteristic for which the absence of jails and the presence of elections are no guarantee.[101] These differences provide a way out of the convergence dilemma confronting those who would compare the American and Soviet systems: The two systems *are* converging (as are most centralized, bureaucratic systems built on industrial, technocratic economic foundations) in that they are, in the broadest sense, both increasingly totalistic. But they remain distinctive inasmuch as the Soviet Union approximates the statist pattern in which revolutionary coercion is used to extend the public sphere into areas previously considered private,[102] while the United States conforms more to a seepage model in which the increasing irrelevance of formal constitutional boundaries coupled with a gradual and largely unperceived evaporation of the distinction between private and public have led to a blending of the two realms favorable to thought and behavior control of a far more subtle kind. The individual personality is submerged in both cases, but in a framework of repressive coercion on the one hand, and in one of consensus, conformity, and legitimacy on the other. Moreover, these two totalist models differ as much from the voluntaristic, communitarian pattern as they do from one another.

In summary, even when we manage to extrapolate from the turgid ambiguities of particular definitions of totalitarianism a paramount concern with the totalistic solution to the problem of scope, very little of analytic importance has been discovered; for totalism is not, as most theorists who use the concept of totalitarianism seem to believe, synonymous with statism. As we have seen, boundaries are not always annihilated by an inexorable mass movement or a monolithic party in control of a public domain gone awry; they may, instead, be absent from the outset either by custom (as in tribal societies) or by choice (as in our above communitarian examples), or they may simply melt away as a function of a natural evolution of political or social processes. To impose modern statist notions in the guise of totalism (or totalitarianism) on voluntaristic, participatory communes like the classical Greek *polis* or the German-Swiss *Gemeinschaft*, or to confound coercive statism and creeping conformity under the rubric of totalism is to perpetrate a kind of conceptual mayhem that leaves the term totalism as impotent analytically as the totalitarian construct it was meant to resuscitate. Even phenomenological definitions are tainted with statist preconceptions, for they invariably identify totalitarianism with a syndrome of objective indicators that measure political coercion, violence, repression, and fear—the chief characteristics not of totalism *per se*, but only of statist totalism.[103] Their preoccupation with empirical indicators leads them, however, to emphasize the measurable end condition of totalism at the expense of the differing historical processes by which it is produced, thus making them peculiarly insensitive to the kinds of distinctions offered here. The observer confronted with three men sitting in a hole may be led by his observations to the conclusion that the three share a common condition. But in reality, if one is there by choice, one by accident, and the third under duress, they may have little in common, the variant meanings of their several conditions being given not so much by their "being-in-a-hole" as by the circumstances under which they came to be in the hole. Indeed, the man in the hole by choice may well feel that he has more in common with those not in the hole by choice than with those who share the hole with him against their will.

Moreover, just as an observer who witnesses one man being coerced into the hole at gunpoint may conclude that others in the hole were similarly coerced, some exponents of totalitarian theory conceive the totalist condition to be an exclusive product of public coercion. This can lead to a convenient logical inversion in which the absence of governmental coercion is taken as proof of the nontotalitarian character of a regime—as in for example, the United States.

Let us, despite the difficulties we have encountered, make the kind of accommodation with totalism that we already have made with totalitarianism; let us assume, that is to say, that we can restrict (stipulatively) the concept of totalism to the critical focus represented by statism, just as we originally isolated totalism as the chief focus and shared concern of the broader concept of totalitarianism. Putting aside the fact that this accommodation would exclude certain kinds of definitions from the outset (thus limiting its utility), and presupposing the agreement of the more recalcitrant of totalitarianism's conceptual advocates, would the accommodation finally provide comparative politics with a tool capable of meaningful analytic discrimination? It probably would not. Even the narrow construction of totalism as statism depends upon a model that is not simply flawed but, in its theoretical implications, politically archaic. It presupposes that the only significant threat to the individual (the private—free—sphere) is the state *qua* state and it thus suggests a permanent condition of being at odds, a condition, as Gierke has said, of "combat in which the Sovereign State and the Sovereign individual contend over the delimitation of the provinces assigned to them by Natural Law."[104] Pursuing Gierke's description, it is a struggle in the course of which "all intermediate groups are first degraded into the position of the more or less arbitrarily fashioned creatures of mere Positive Law, and in the end are obliterated."[105] The resulting condition, clearly favoring public power, facilitates "the penetration of the total state into every pore of the 'atomized' society,"[106] and thus gives rise to statist totalism; or so we are led to believe. But can we realistically expect this beguiling but antiquarian metaphor—intended as a nineteenth-century explanation of the transition from the organic social corporatism of the High Middle Ages to the mechanistic political atomism of the early modern period (in thinkers like Spinoza and Hobbes)

—to provide an appropriate framework for modern political analysis? The unhappy truth is that the classic liberal paradigm conceived in terms of an abstract dualism between the atomized individual and the monolithic state has never been very useful in concrete analysis, and is almost entirely without relevance to the problems of contemporary politics; yet, despite overt rejection by most political scientists, the model has been covertly revived in the concept of totalitarianism (in the statist element), perhaps because its pertinence to totalism has been largely unrecognized and its moribund conceptual antecedents thus mostly overlooked or ignored.

The model itself has, of course, been explicitly challenged on several different grounds. From the inception of modern political philosophy, theorists have been confronted with the problem of locating "society" on their new two-dimensional political maps. Some (for example, Hobbes) circumvented the issue by rendering society and the state synonymous, but subsequent commentators have had to grapple with the more sophisticated analytic legacy of Locke, in which society is distinguished both from government (narrowly construed) and from the private realm (embodied in the state of nature).[107] Is society to be viewed as public or private? Does it partake of freedom (the defining characteristic of the atomized individual) or power (the essential attribute of the state)? To the extent that its boundaries are deemed coterminous with those of the state, or it eschews completely the requisites of public power, its abstract presence can be tolerated within the framework of a public-private dualism. But, if it suggests the private control of power (by social groups meant to de-atomize and lend organic identity to the private sphere) that has potentially a public usefulness, the simplistic dualism inhering in the totalist paradigm breaks down. Even in the last century, the suspicion that power could be a function of social and economic elites operating outside the formal public domain in a sphere neither public nor private (in the Hobbesian sense) was widespread, not exclusively in the economic determinism of Malthus, Ricardo, and Marx, but also in the sociological theory of elitism that came to fruition in Mosca and Pareto. In the present century, it has been generally acknowledged that power can be a function not simply of a formally defined public realm but also of social and economic forces that stalk, but are not part of, the private realm and that individuals can be victimized by "private" monopolies beyond the pale of public regulation or control. Indeed, because the state is politically controllable and its activities are visible, its threats to personal liberty are, in some ways, less pernicious than those emanating from unrecognized influence-sources operating under assumed but totally unreal conditions of equality in a supposedly fragmented and pluralistic private sphere. To the extent that such forces come to dominate both the private and the public spheres, the public-private distinction and debate about boundaries become correspondingly irrelevant.

The liberal faith in the private-public paradigm has not expired easily, however. Arguments that undermine faith in the sanctity (even the existence) of the private sphere are often written off as being motivated by politics, polemics, or bombast—sometimes also being dismissed as Marxist.[108] Of particular comfort to those who would preserve the classic paradigm upon which totalism rests has been the theory of pluralism, which, in its most rudimentary form, may be understood as an attempt to salvage the political innocence of the private sphere by substituting system components without changing system rules. In the new format, the private realm is comprised not of free and equal individuals (whose role, as described by traditional constitutionalists, has been, it is conceded, discredited) but of diversified and competing interest-aggregates (for example, pressure groups); these social groups are potentially equal (in that, in a pluralistic society, their influence is a function of intensity) and, as the new repositories of social freedom, deserve from the state the same guarantees of "hands off" (*laissez-faire*) as were once accorded the individual.[109] The duty of the public realm is to preserve the integrity and freedom of the constituents of the private realm (that is, these groups) whose aggregated particular interests together constitute the only meaningful public interest worthy of discussion.[110]

In spite, then, of the decline of liberal individualism as a credible descriptive framework for politics, the theory of pluralism has enabled exponents of the statist version of totalitarianism to continue to identify "totalitarian" regimes with statist oppression of private liberties—understood now, however, in terms of groups rather than of individuals. Totalism becomes an antonym not of individualism but of pluralism.[111] It is unlikely, however, that the pluralist paradigm for liberal dualism will be any more enduring analytically than its individualistic predecessor. A tide of criticism is rising—not only from the troubled waters of the American left,[112] but also from the respectable mainstream of contemporary political thought—against the uncertain foundations of the pluralist superstructure. The pluralists see in pressure politics a substitute for traditional democratic rulership in an era where direct participation by individuals is unfeasible and political influence difficult to obtain. To think, however, that the pressure system is representative of the whole community that comprises the private sphere is, as E. E. Schattschneider points out, "a myth fostered by the universalizing tendency of modern group theories. Pressure politics is a selective process ill-designed to serve diffuse interests. The system is skewed, loaded and unbalanced in favor of a fraction of a minority."[113] Pressure groups, as critics of pluralist theory like Henry Kariel persuasively insist, are not simply expressions of relatively equal particular interests in a relationship of perfect competition; they may be manifestations of major social and economic forces capable of manipulating both private and public interests for their own objectives. Where these conditions obtain, the problem is "not how to strengthen the hierarchies of organized private power but rather how to control them."[114] Pluralists, like their liberal predecessors, assume that the primary danger to freedom of action for individuals and groups lies in centralized political power, and that pluralist freedom and statist totalism are, consequently, natural antitheses. But "the organizations which the early theorists of pluralism relied upon to sustain the individual against a unified government have themselves become oligarchically governed hierarchies, and now place unjustifiable limits on constitutional democracy."[115] There is little, then, in pluralist theory, to inspire confidence either in the reliability of the statist-totalist core of the concept totalitarianism or in the liberal paradigm upon which it theoretically depends.

Ironically, the work currently being done not only in areas like public administration, decisional theory, and attitudinal survey research but also in group theory itself[116] claims to be fully emancipated from the institutional and legalistic excesses of the liberal German tradition of *Rechtswissenschaft* out of which American political science originally sprang. Yet, in the vital area of comparative political analysis, political scientists continue to employ at least one concept that, though it is new as a term, derives its analytic significance from these very sources. Totalitarianism has a generally accepted meaning only insofar as we focus on the totalistic element in it, conceived in narrow statist terms; statism, in turn, makes sense only if we presuppose—in the manner of traditional liberal theory—a dualistic cleavage between abstract public and private spheres. But this is precisely the kind of presupposition that a rejection of the liberal philosophy of the state as a descriptive instrument of analysis disallows. The arduous and unrewarding task of uncovering foundations for the totalitarian construct results only in the discovery that what meager foundations there are have been built on the shifting sands of a theory of politics that can no longer carry the weight resting upon it; (this may mean that there is an element of wise prudence in the reluctance of exponents of the totalitarian construct to explore the bases of their notion in theory).

Whether we take the concept, with all of its ambiguities and contradictions, at face value or seek to identify common roots and concerns in divergent definitions, it is difficult to find a convincing justification for the presence of totalitarianism in the vocabulary of comparative political analysis. Taken at face value, our multiple definitions are sufficiently contradictory to warrant the charge that totalitarianism has no specific meaning at all, and is thus, for purposes of analysis, quite useless. If, to avoid this skeptical conclusion, we postulate (on the rather precarious basis of a generous reading of our multiple interpretations) a common emphasis on totalism, we are still confronted with at least three quite distinctive forms of totalism that the concept totalitarianism is thus guilty of concealing. If, finally, to put an end to these escalating ambiguities, we restrict totalism (and thus totalitarianism) to its statist variant, a different but equally troublesome weakness is revealed: the dependence of the concept on a theoretical perspective few political scientists regard as relevant to the problems of modern politics and which those who do themselves use the concept often reject. There are a number of major political constructs (like democracy or influence) that are controversial both in meaning and in application, but totalitarianism is exceptional even in their company. Unexamined, in its multiple definitional manifestations, totalitarianism lacks coherence, clarity, and a single meaning. Examined and uniformly defined, it becomes conceptually archaic; it can purchase coherence only by surrendering its relevance; it can buy uniformity of meaning only at the price of its usefulness. In either case, the analytic utility of totalitarianism is severely circumscribed, and the argument for retaining it in the conceptual vocabulary rendered correspondingly untenable.

Given these fundamental limitations, we cannot agree with those who, like Robert Tucker or A. G. Meyer, contend that, despite its flaws, totalitarianism is a necessary construct. To argue that the term is too firmly embedded in the public consciousness to be successfully extirpated is unconvincing, for unlike such comparable notions as democracy or dictatorship, totalitarianism has no sanctimonious pedigree in popular history or customary usage. Emulating the worst in professional usage, those statesmen and citizens who use the term in everyday parlance are inclined toward an emotivism that is politically perilous as well as philosophically misleading.[117] As Sigmund Neumann notes in the passage with which this essay began, in addition to being disfunctional, the use of outdated or ambiguous concepts can be exceedingly dangerous. When General de Gaulle cautions the Soviet Union not to follow a policy of "crushing totalitarianism" in Czechoslovakia,[118] or former President Johnson defends the American presence in Vietnam by reference to his refusal to allow men "to be delivered over to totalitarianism,"[119] public fears may be effectively (if perilously) aroused, but little of substance is communicated to subject or citizen, to ally or enemy.

We are not so foolish as to think that by standing in an analytic wilderness and crying "abandon the concept of totalitarianism!" a radical change in professional usage can be achieved (or even initiated). Something may be accomplished, however, if an increasing number of students of comparative politics can be persuaded to examine in greater depth the theoretical implications of the concepts, the dimension labels, and the constructs they presently employ with such unwarranted assurance. A carefully and critically nurtured language of comparative political analysis will leave little room for concepts like totalitarianism; and if neglected with sufficient vigor, it is not impossible that the totalitarian construct will be overtaken, if not by oblivion, at least by creeping desuetude.

NOTES

1. S. Neumann, *Permanent Revolution: Totalitarianism in the Age of International Civil War* (2d ed.; New York: Frederick A. Praeger, 1965), pp. xviii-xix. Neumann merely reiterated what in fact had been perceived by political scientists for a long time; as early as 1885, Woodrow Wilson cautioned that "names are much more persistent than the functions upon which they were originally bestowed . . . institutions constantly undergo essential alterations of character, whilst retaining the names conferred upon them in their first estate." *Congressional Government* (Cleveland, Ohio: World Publishing, Meridian ed., 1956), p. 28. Nor did Neumann coin the term itself, which came into use—according to the Oxford English Dictionary—in the late 1920's.

2. A few critical studies have finally emerged in recent years that attempt to examine totalitarianism relatively systematically. Among them are Herbert J. Spiro's contribution to the *International Encyclopedia of the Social Sciences* entitled "Totalitarianism: Critique of a Concept"; Alexander J. Groth's "The 'Isms' in Totalitarianism," *American Political Science Review*, LVIII, No. 4 (1964), pp. 888-901, which represents only a limited critique of the concept as applied to particular (Communist and Fascist) regimes; Robert C. Tucker's "Toward a Comparative Politics of Movement-Regimes," *American Political Science Review*, LV, No. 2 (1961), pp. 281-89, as well as his "The Dictator and Totalitarianism," *World Politics*, XVII, No. 4 (1965), pp. 555-83; and a review essay by Robert Burrowes entitled "Totalitarianism: The Revised Standard Edition," *World Politics*, XXI, No. 2 (1969), pp. 272-89. These pieces, and most comparable studies, tend to address themselves to particular kinds of definitions or to usage found to be especially objectionable by the authors rather than to the wider question of the place of totalitarianism in political philosophy and comparative political analysis. Daniel Bell's "Ten Theses in Search of Reality: the Prediction of Soviet Behavior in the Social Sciences," *World Politics*, X, No. 2 (1958), pp. 327-65, uses a much broader perspective, but one that, unfortunately, touches only incidentally on the concept of totalitarianism. The most provocative piece in the area of methodology is the recent study by Frederic J. Fleron, Jr., "Soviet Area Studies and the Social Sciences: Some Methodological Problems in Communist Studies," *Soviet Studies*, XIX, No. 3 (1968), pp. 313-339. Fleron's work, although excessively linguistic in orientation, settles felicitously on totalitarianism as its primary illustrative focus and thus provides the student of the concept with numerous insights. Many of the methodological issues raised by Fleron are treated quite separately from the problem of totalitarianism in Arthur Kalleberg, "The Logic of Comparison: A Methodological Note on the Comparative Study of Political Systems," *World Politics*, XIX, No. 1 (1966), pp. 69-82.

3. The term is almost more popular with statesmen, policy-makers, and phrase-makers than with professional social scientists. The newspapers are full

of examples, two of which are cited here: from former President Lyndon B. Johnson, "no man, whatever the pigmentation of their skins [sic], should ever be delivered over to totalitarianism" (*The New York Times*, October 26, 1967); and from General Charles de Gaulle: "We made it clear to the great Russian people that the whole of Europe expected much better things of it than a policy of isolation and putting its satellites in chains within the confines of a crushing totalitarianism" (*The New York Times*, September 10, 1968). For a critique of the ideological implications of such usage see Herbert J. Spiro and Benjamin R. Barber, "The Concept of Totalitarianism as the Foundation of American Counter-Ideology in the Cold War," paper delivered to the 1967 Annual Meeting of the American Political Science Association. Professor Fleron comments in this context "I should guess that if we knew enough of the psychology of research we would find that there are those who wish to retain 'totalitarianism' in studying communism because of its negative connotations. This may be one of the reasons why the definition of 'totalitarianism' is constantly revised so that as the Soviet Union changes (e.g., away from the overt use of terror) the concept can still be used to denote that system. Various acrobatics are performed with the concept (e.g., 'mature totalitarianism') so that we can continue to pin a 'boo' label on a 'boo' system of government." *Op. cit.*, p. 339, n. 84.

4. J. D. Mabbott, *The State and the Citizen* (London: Grew Arrow, 1958), p. 61: "The opposite of Totalitarianism is neither democracy nor beneficent law, but *laissez-faire*."

5. Hannah Arendt, *The Origins of Totalitarianism*, Rev. ed. (Cleveland, Ohio: World Publishing, Meridian ed., 1958), pp. 459 *et passim*.

6. John Kautsky, *Political Change in Underdeveloped Countries: Nationalism and Communism* (New York: John Wiley & Sons, 1962), p. 90. A similar complaint is voiced by R. Robinson in his review of Karl Popper's *The Open Society and Its Enemies*: "I still do not know what [Popper] or anyone else means by Totalitarianism." *Philosophical Review*, LX, No. 4 (October, 1951), p. 503.

7. See Spiro, *op. cit.*, and Michael Curtis' contribution in this volume.

8. See, for example, Rudolf Wurlitzer, "Review of Frederick Exley's 'A Fan's Notes,' " *The New Republic*, November 2, 1968: "Occasionally the style is forced and excessive, but this seems more a maneuver against the totalitarianism of the first person than an indulgent aesthetic."

9. See, for example, Arendt, *op. cit.*, pp. 341 ff.

10. See, for example, C. W. Cassinelli, "The Totalitarian Party," *Journal of Politics*, XXIV, No. 1 (1962); and B. E. Lippincott, *Democracy's Dilemma: The Totalitarian Party in a Free Society* (New York: Ronald Press, 1965).

11. See, for example, Tucker, "The Dictator and Totalitarianism," *op. cit.*

12. For example, Gabriel Almond explains the process of what he calls "totalitarian communication" in *The Politics of the Developing Areas* (Princeton, N.J.: Princeton University Press, 1960), p. 47.

13. There is an extensive literature devoted to "totalitarian ideas," which includes such classics as Karl Popper's *The Open Society and Its Enemies* (4th

ed.; Princeton, N.J.: Princeton University Press, 1963), and J. L. Talmon's *The Origins of Totalitarian Democracy* (New York: Frederick A. Praeger, 1961); the literature has grown rapidly in recent years and now encompasses such studies as Robert E. MacMaster's *Danilevsky: A Russian Totalitarian Philosopher* (Cambridge, Mass.: Harvard University Press, 1967); A. James Gregor's *Contemporary Radical Ideologies: Totalitarian Thought in the Twentieth Century* (New York: Random House, 1968); and a peculiar work by Rabbi Arthur Hertzberg, which attributes to such *Philosophes* as Diderot and Voltaire responsibility for modern anti-Semitism and totalitarianism, *The French Enlightenment and the Jews* (New York: Columbia University Press, 1968).

14. See Lippincott, *op. cit.*, for a statement of this argument.

15. Most recent studies of the Soviet Union have utilized the concept of totalitarianism as a primary instrument of analysis; see, *inter alia*, the works of Adam B. Ulam, Bertram D. Wolfe, Barrington Moore, Jr., Frederich Schuman, Merle Fainsod, Alex Inkeles, Z. K. Brzezinski, and W. W. Rostow. With the exception of a few British Sovietologists (e.g., the late Isaac Deutscher or Leonard Schapiro), even those political scientists who have reservations about the term continue, however reluctantly, to employ it; Robert Tucker, though critical of the concept, is unwilling to dispense with it in the articles cited above, and A. G. Meyer—perhaps the most convincing American critic of totalitarianism as a route to adequate analysis of Soviet politics—nevertheless cannot quite bring himself to break entirely with conventional usage; see his *The Soviet Political System* (New York: Random House, 1966), pp. 467-76. So pervasive has American usage become that independent Communists in Eastern Europe and the Soviet Union have begun to frame their critical strictures in the language of totalitarian theory. Prior to the Soviet invasion of Czechoslovakia, for example, a Czech philosopher (and member of the Communist party) is reported to have urged his fellow countrymen to move "from a totalitarian society to an open society" (*The New York Times*, April 14, 1968); following the invasion, a former major-general of the Soviet Army purportedly denounced publicly the "totalitarianism that hides behind the mask of so-called democracy" (*The New York Times*, November 15, 1968). Such usage is no doubt predominantly emotive, for there is not even agreement among American students of the Soviet Union about the institutions to which the term can be most appropriately applied. Soviet area specialists have differentiated at least three discrete periods of Soviet political life (Leninist, Stalinist, and post-Stalinist) and have expended considerable time and energy debating the suitability of the term to each. Although many experts have restricted their use of totalitarianism to the Stalinist period, in his contribution to this volume, Carl J. Friedrich argues that Stalinism is an "aberration" from the normal totalitarian pattern. Efforts to dissociate post-Stalinist Russia from the totalitarian model (e.g., Isaac Deutscher's *Russia in Transition* [Rev. ed., New York: Grove Press, 1960]) have had to contend with ongoing Russian intervention in Eastern Europe—Hungary in 1956, or Czechoslovakia in 1968—although Soviet policy in this region is probably fully explicable in

terms of national interest, power politics, and gaming models, which, without resort to totalitarian theory, can point to traditional Czarist interests in Eastern Europe, to Russian distrust of Germany, or to America's inability to respond because of its East Asian entanglement as factors contributing to the present situation.

16. Although Nazi Germany has been treated by Sigmund Neumann, Hannah Arendt, and many others as even more prototypical than the Soviet Union, historians of the Nazi epoch have been somewhat more reluctant to use totalitarianism in connection with it, both because of the short-lived and highly personalistic character of the regime and because of its status as a dead system; historians like William Shirer have thus written accounts without resorting to totalitarian theory (see *The Rise and Fall of the Third Reich* [New York: Simon and Schuster, 1959]). But, if the history of Germany has done without the concept, the theory of nazism has not; see, for example, Hans Buchheim, *Totalitarian Rule: Its Nature and Characteristics* (Middletown, Conn.: Wesleyan University Press, 1968) or A. James Gregor, *op. cit.*, for recent examples.

17. The best example here is perhaps Dante Germino's *The Italian Fascist Party in Power: A Study in Totalitarian Rule* (Minneapolis: University of Minnesota Press, 1959); Mediterranean fascism has, however, proved less amenable to classification under the totalitarian rubric than its Nordic cousin; for a discussion that moves beyond debate about the vicissitudes of the Latin temperament see Alexander Groth, *op. cit.* Among students of autocratic systems, only Gregor has insisted that Italian—rather than German or Russian—fascism is "paradigmatic of twentieth-century totalitarianism." *Op. cit.*, p. 336.

18. Peter Wiles, "Comment on Tucker's 'Movement-Regimes,' " *American Political Science Review*, LV, No. 2 (1961), pp. 290 ff.

19. Barrington Moore, Jr., *Political Power and Social Theory* (New York: Harper & Row, 1965), p. 54.

20. Franz Neumann, *The Democratic and Authoritarian State* (Chicago: The Free Press of Glencoe, 1957), p. 246.

21. An extensive literature has grown out of Karl Popper's study of Plato as a totalitarian in the first volume of his *Open Society and Its Enemies*. See, for example, John Wild, *Plato and His Modern Enemies* (Chicago: Chicago University Press, 1953) and T. L. Thorsen (ed.), *Plato: Totalitarian or Democrat?* (Englewood Cliffs, N.J.: Prentice-Hall, 1963).

22. For an interesting critical discussion of conceptual problems in the study of modern China, see D. B. Bubrow, "Old Dragons in New Models," *World Politics*, XIX, No. 2 (1967), pp. 306-19.

23. Moore, *op. cit.*, p. 40. Moore's treatment is clearly influenced by Karl Wittfogels' classic study *Oriental Despotism* (New Haven: Yale University Press, 1957).

24. A course given by Michael Zuckerman at the University of Pennsylvania in 1967 carried the title "The United States as a Totalitarian Society." Aside from its pejorative implications, the appellation's appropriateness to

America has been discussed in the "convergence thesis" literature examined below; see notes 56-57, *infra*.

25. The inclusion on this list of the United States in the 1840's is bizarre enough to warrant an explanation: Barrington Moore, Jr. depicts de Tocqueville's study of American political life as "a penetrating description of the mechanics of popular totalitarianism," which, Moore thus indicates, emerged in the United States "two generations . . . before big industry would even begin to dominate the American scene"; *op. cit.*, pp. 83-85. He is, of course, only examining totalitarian *elements* in preindustrial societies, and his position is, thus, relativistic.

26. " . . . there have been times when Christianity was dominated by totalitarian ideas . . . and, in another form, it may come again." Popper, *op. cit.*, I, p. 104.

27. F. Neumann, *op. cit.*

28. See John Kautsky, *op. cit.*; or Barrington Moore, Jr., *Social Origins of Dictatorship and Democracy* (Boston: Beacon Press, 1966); a number of other development theorists use the concept with less conscious rigor. See, for example, G. Almond and J. Coleman (eds.), *op. cit.*, pp. 40 *et passim*; or David Apter, *The Politics of Modernization* (Chicago: University of Chicago Press, 1965), pp. 301, 388 ff.

29. Hobbes's political system is associated, by indirection, with what Lewis S. Feuer calls "the seventeenth century version of totalitarian ideology" in his *Spinoza and the Rise of Liberalism* (Boston: Beacon Press, 1964), p. 193.

30. Moore, *Social Origins, op. cit.*, pp. 288 ff.

31. Moore, *Political Power, op. cit.*, pp. 59 ff.

32. Although he has the good sense to set it off with quotation marks, F. L. Ganshof nonetheless speaks of "the 'totalitarian' character of the subordination of the vassal" in depicting the feudal relationship under Charlemagne. *Feudalism* (London: Longmans, Green, 1964), p. 31. Such examples as those given here could no doubt be infinitely multiplied by a careful survey of the modern literature of politics. One wonders if *any* regime would ultimately escape being labeled totalitarian by some particular writer with some particular definition in mind.

33. See *infra*, p. 126. Compare also with the definition in C. J. Friedrich and Z. K. Brzezinski, *Totalitarian Dictatorship and Autocracy*, Rev. ed. (New York: Frederick A. Praeger, 1967).

34. Frederick Hayek is perhaps supremely guilty in this respect—see his arid but influential polemic *The Road to Serfdom* (Chicago: University of Chicago Press, 1944)—but he is closely trailed by Karl Popper. Even the more concise and systematic writers (like Hannah Arendt, Barrington Moore, Jr.,or Adam Ulam) use their central conceptual term with an uncomfortably careless lack of specificity.

35. For example, Hans Buchheim's definition, which incorporates an indicator called "the creeping rape of man," is omitted for this reason; interested parties can consult Buchheim, *op. cit.*

36. C. J. Friedrich and Z. K. Brzezinski have constructed their own

definitional taxonomy for totalitarianism, to which the following can be compared; *op. cit.*, pp. 15-21.

37. Hannah Arendt, *op. cit.*, p. 466; see p. 460 for an elaboration. The citation does not do justice to the sweeping scope and depth of vision of Arendt's investigation of totalitarianism—pursued in her *Eichmann in Jerusalem: A Report on the Banality of Evil* (New York: Viking Press, 1963)—but her persistent emphasis on terror makes her definition archetypical of the terror formula employed by commentators like Adam B. Ulam in his "The Russian Political System," in S. Beer and A. B. Ulam (eds.), *Patterns of Government* (New York: Random House, 1962), and (surprisingly) Herbert Marcuse, both in his *Soviet Marxism: A Critical Analysis* (New York: Columbia University Press, 1958) and in his more recent *One-Dimensional Man* (Boston: Beacon Press, 1964), where the coercive, as against the manipulative, form of totalitarianism is characterized as the "terroristic political coordination of society." See p. 3. For Marcuse's position see *infra*, n. 56 on convergence theory.

38. Z. K. Brzezinski, *Ideology and Power in Soviet Politics*, Rev. ed. (New York: Frederick A. Praeger, 1967), pp. 46-47. Brzezinski's views, like those of many students of totalitarianism, have undergone considerable change since his collaboration with Carl J. Friedrich more than a decade ago; the citation is, for this reason, taken from his most recent work. As will be seen, it has little in common with the point of view of his earlier collaborator. For an even earlier view, see Brzezinski's *The Permanent Purge* (Cambridge, Mass.: Harvard University Press, 1956).

39. Karl Deutsch, "Cracks in the Monolith: Possibilities and Patterns of Disintegration in Totalitarian Systems," in C. J. Friedrich (ed.), *Totalitarianism: Proceedings of a Conference Held at the American Academy of Arts and Sciences* (Cambridge, Mass.: Harvard University Press, 1954), pp. 308-9 ff.

40. Harry Eckstein and David E. Apter, *Comparative Politics: A Reader* (New York: The Free Press, 1963), p. 434.

41. Frederick A. Hayek, *op. cit.*, Chap. VII. Although Hayek's polemic cannot be taken seriously by social scientists, his identification of totalitarianism with economic control represents a widely shared position, especially in England where, among others, Karl Popper and J. D. Mabbott (the former approvingly, the latter disapprovingly) concur in Hayek's general point of view about the meaning of totalitarianism.

42. John H. Kautsky, *op. cit.*, p. 91.

43. Barrington Moore, Jr., *Political Power, op. cit.*, pp. 74-75.

44. Franz Neumann, *op. cit.*, p. 245. Neumann also provides a set of objective indicators, which includes the prevalence of terror; for Neumann, however, terror is not an exclusive preoccupation, as it is for Hannah Arendt or Adam B. Ulam.

45. Sigmund Neumann, *op. cit.*, p. xii.

46. Karl Popper, *op. cit.*, pp. 1-2 *et passim*. Because Popper never clearly defines totalitarianism, I have simply noted the three critical phrases that recur in connection with it throughout his study.

47. J. L. Talmon, *op. cit.*, pp. 2-3.

48. Z. K. Brzezinski, *Ideology and Power, op. cit.*, p. 46. Brzezinski's own definition is, of course, more essentialist than phenomenological in character.

49. Friedrich and Brzezinski, *op. cit.*, p. 21.

50. Karl Deutsch, *op. cit.*, p. 497.

51. Arthur Banks and Robert Textor, *A Cross-Polity Survey* (Cambridge, Mass.: MIT Press, 1963), p. 83. Totalitarianism is employed there as part of a trichotomy (including authoritarianism and constitutionalism) defining the "constitutional status of present regimes," which, in turn, is one of fifty-seven "raw characteristics" used to classify nations.

52. R. J. Rummel, "The Relationship Between National Attributes and Foreign Conflict Behavior," in J. D. Singer (ed.), *Quantitative International Politics* (New York: The Free Press, 1968), p. 207.

53. "A real definition is a statement of the 'essential attributes' or the 'essential nature' of a given entity." F. J. Fleron, Jr., *op. cit.*, p. 324. For a linguistic critique of such definitions see also T. D. Weldon's classic, *The Vocabulary of Politics* (London: Penguin Books, 1953).

54. Brzezinski, *Ideology and Power, op. cit.*, p. 47. Despite their early collaboration, Friedrich and Brzezinski appear to have moved in increasingly incompatible directions in the last decade; their present positions have little in common.

55. Eckstein and Apter, *op. cit.*, p. 437. Gregor echoes this position in his contention that "some of the principal species traits of totalitarianism are already common to all industrially advanced countries." *Op. cit.*, p. 339.

56. This is the argument intimated by Barrington Moore, Jr., when he asserts that "both Western liberalism and communism have begun to display symptoms of historical obsolescence. As successful doctrines they have started to turn into ideologies that justify and conceal numerous forms of repression." *Social Origins, op. cit.*, p. 508. Herbert Marcuse is less hesitant in elaborating the argument, contending that "by virtue of the way it has organized its technological base, contemporary industrial society tends to be totalitarian. For 'totalitarian' is . . . also a non-terroristic economic-technical coordination which operates through the manipulation of needs by vested interests. . . . Not only a specific form of government or party rule makes for totalitarianism, but also a specific system of production and distribution which may well be compatible with a 'pluralism' of parties, newspapers, 'countervailing powers,' etc." *One-Dimensional Man, op. cit.*, p. 3.

57. A. G. Meyer, for example, avoids the term totalitarian, favoring, instead, the term "bureaucratic," which leads him to the conclusion that "the Soviet political system, in its structure and functioning, in the character of the people active in it and even in its basic goals, is quite similar to some social organizations with which we in the United States are very familiar . . . the Soviet way of life therefore is similar in many essentials to the American way of life." *Op. cit.*, p. 475. Emphasis on such rival concepts as bureaucracy has led a number of political scientists into reassessing traditional terms like totalitarianism, Communism, or Stalinism. A recent review of A. Doak Barnett's *Cadres, Bureaucracy, and Political Power in Communist China* allows

that "If Mr. Barnett had eliminated the words 'China' and 'Communist' from the text . . . this book would read like any of several standard works in the field of political administration. Before 1966 at least, the bureaucrat in China mirrored the style and outlook of bureaucrats everywhere." John W. Lewis, "The Chinese Bureaucrat," *The New Republic*, December 16, 1967. In a similar vein, Jean Edward Smith makes it the thesis of his article "The Red Prussianism of the German Democratic Republic," *Political Science Quarterly*, LXXXII, No. 3 (1967), pp. 368-69, that "times have changed; the mould of Stalinism most frequently associated with the German Democratic Republic has never had significant validity." The convergence thesis has not gone unchallenged, however. Z. K. Brzezinski and S. P. Huntington disputed it in detail in their *Political Power: USA/USSR* (New York: Viking, 1964), although much of the evidence they adduce points to similarities rather than contrasts in the American and Soviet systems. Their case against convergence rests finally on dubious prognostication about the "path of development" anticipated for the two systems; see, for example, p. 436. Brzezinski later unwittingly contradicted this position in an article rooted in technological determinism treating America as a "technotronic" society whose affairs "do not fit established categories of analysis." If applied to the Soviet Union and other developed, industrial (and postindustrial) nations, this position would compel acceptance of the convergence argument. See "The American Tradition," *The New Republic*, December 23, 1967.

58. See, for example, Fleron, *op. cit.*, p. 324. Ideological and emotive overtones taint even phenomenological usage, a fact that leads one to wonder why social scientists do not simply discard totalitarianism the way natural scientists have rejected such false-associational terms as "phlogiston," "ether," and "epicycle." Since its origins are in stipulation rather than customary usage, the arguments Tucker and Fleron make about its wide popular acceptance are beside the point. To withdraw a term that has not succeeded in fulfilling the purposes for which it was stipulatively introduced cannot be considered robbing the people of ancient and revered semantic symbols. (See *supra* for an elaboration on this point.)

59. Leo Strauss, *What is Political Philosophy* (Chicago: The Free Press of Glencoe, 1959), p. 21. Relevant to this style of criticism is the growing body of literature applying both Marxist and non-Marxist theories of the sociology of knowledge to American political science. See, for example, R. P. Wolff, Barrington Moore, Jr., and Herbert Marcuse, *A Critique of Pure Tolerance* (Boston: Beacon Press, 1965), or C. Wright Mills, *The Sociological Imagination* (New York: Oxford University Press, 1959).

60. F. Neumann, *op. cit.*, pp. 243 ff.

61. Eckstein and Apter, *op. cit.*, p. 435.

62. F. Neumann, *op. cit.* Brzezinski follows a more peculiar pattern: "Totalitarianism, therefore, has to be considered as a new form of government falling into the general classification of dictatorship" (*Ideology and Power, op. cit.*, p. 46), a strange formula, which puts totalitarianism into the general class of dictatorship while simultaneously insisting on its uniqueness.

63. Friedrich and Brzezinski, *op. cit.*, p. 15.

64. *Ibid.*, pp. 15 and 24.

65. Popper, *op. cit.*, p. 1.

66. Tucker, "Movement-Regimes," *op. cit.*, p. 281.

67. Meyer, *op. cit.*, p. 471.

68. Moore, *Political Power, op. cit.*, p. 74. The contention generally arises out of an attempt to apply totalitarianism to the political attributes (e.g., single-party rule, censorship, terror, et cetera) of regimes that are patently preindustrial—that is, developing systems such as Ghana under Nkrumah, Indonesia under Sukarno, or Cuba under Castro.

69. "A good comparative concept should perform a dual discriminating function: it should direct attention to the ways in which similar phenomena differ, and simultaneously to the ways in which differing phenomena resemble each other. I have suggested that the concept of totalitarianism is deficient in the former respect. . . . I must now extend the argument by suggesting that it also fails to direct attention to significant resemblances." Tucker, "Movement-Regimes," *op. cit.*, p. 283.

70. Bertram D. Wolfe, *Communist Totalitarianism* (Boston: Beacon Press, 1956), p. 261.

71. *Ibid.*

72. Talmon, *op. cit.*, p. 1.

73. *Ibid.*, pp. 6-7.

74. See, for example, Alexis de Tocqueville, *Democracy in America* (New York: Random House, Vintage ed., 1961), I, pp. 264 ff.

75. Ortega y Gassett, *The Revolt of the Masses* (New York: W. W. Norton, 1957), p. 17. See also pp. 94-96. "Hyperdemocracy" makes an attractive synonym for totalitarianism.

76. L. S. Feuer, *Spinoza and the Rise of Liberalism* (Boston: Beacon Press, 1964), p. 106.

77. See, for example, William Kornhauser, *The Politics of Mass Society* (Chicago: The Free Press of Glencoe, 1959).

78. See, for example, Eric Hoffer, *The True Believer* (New York: Harper & Bros., 1951).

79. For a modern discussion from the kind of Marxist viewpoint that first inspired the controversy over "alienation," see Stanley W. Moore, *The Critique of Capitalist Democracy* (New York: Paine-Whitman, 1957), especially Chap. 4. Most of the discussion today is written from the perspective of psychology; e.g., Eric Fromm, *Escape From Freedom* (New York: Avon Books, 1968), or T. W. Adorno *et al.*, *The Authoritarian Personality* (New York: Harper & Bros., 1950).

80. Eckstein and Apter, *op. cit.*, p. 437.

81. Nomenclature varies among classical writers: Aristotle's classification is monarchy, aristocracy, and polity, and their perversions are tyranny, oligarchy, and democracy.

82. Isaiah Berlin, *Two Concepts of Liberty* (New York: Oxford University Press, 1958), p. 14.

83. Factor analysis is an instrument particularly suitable to this task. It is a mistake, however, to assume that, because terms are used in factor analysis to label concrete empirical indicators, their theoretical antecedents are unimportant. Unless arbitrary labels are invented, the relationship between a particular set of indicators and the term identifying it is bound to be mutual in character; indeed, the constellations into which individual indicators are grouped are determined in part by the conceptual nature of the dimensions such constellations are intended to define (unless, again, it is argued that indicators are randomly grouped).

84. "[T]otalitarian societies appear to be merely exaggerations, but nonetheless logical exaggerations, of the technological state of modern society." Friedrich and Brzezinski, *op. cit.*, p. 24. This argument is more apposite to the means by which totalitarianism is purportedly achieved than to the end condition.

85. As it has been used by R. J. Lifton in his *Thought Reform and the Psychology of Totalism* (New York: W. W. Norton, 1963), and as it is usually understood by students of totalitarianism; see, for example, C. J. Friedrich, *infra*, pp. 133-35, or Friedrich and Brzezinski, *op. cit.*, p. 17.

86. Talmon, *op. cit.*, pp. 2-3.

87. F. Neumann, *op. cit.* p. 245.

88. Eckstein and Apter, *op. cit.*, p. 434.

89. R. Bauer, A. Inkeles, and C. Kluckhohn, *How the Soviet System Works* (Cambridge, Mass.: Harvard University Press, 1959), p. 20.

90. Friedrich and Brzezinski, *op. cit.*, p. 17.

91. Hans Kelsen, *The Political Theory of Bolshevism* (Berkeley, Calif.: University of California Press, 1959), p. 6. Numerous other examples can be found; for example, Peter Wiles' definition of a totalitarian system as "a type of regime under which the state governs the whole life of each of its individual subjects in all respects." *Op. cit.*, p. 290. Or A. G. Meyer's observation that "those political systems are totalitarian which seek to politicize all human endeavor, to organize and plan all human relationships." *Op. cit.*, p. 471.

92. A glance at the range of authors in Notes 86-91 will perhaps persuade those who are dubious on this point.

93. This assumption is for many axiomatic; Theodore Lowi, for example, believes that "in a democracy there is a tendency toward expansion of the public sphere." *Private Life and Public Order* (New York: W. W. Norton, 1968), p. viii.

94. Talmon, *op. cit.*, pp. 1-2. Or perhaps his logic flows in the other direction; in either case, no empirical or theoretical evidence that warrants an uncritical acceptance of the implicit relationship is presented.

95. "What all Greek philosophers, no matter how opposed to *polis* life, took for granted is that freedom is exclusively located in the political realm, that necessity is primarily a pre-political phenomenon, characteristic of the private household organization." Hannah Arendt, *The Human Condition* (New York: Doubleday, Anchor ed., 1959), p. 29.

96. Lowi, *op. cit.*, p. vii. This tension can be resolved, from the perspective of liberalism, only by the complete noninvolvement of the state in affairs other than those dictated by its watchdog functions as guardian of the private sphere and guarantor of liberty. Not all modern liberal theorists fail to distinguish between communitarianism and totalitarianism, but most seem persuaded that there are few differences between them. Rousseau's liberal detractors thus remain almost as numerous as Plato's. Bertrand Russell assures us, for example, that "Hitler is an outcome of Rousseau"—a charge which would probably have pleased Hitler even less than Rousseau; *History of Western Philosophy* (New York: Simon & Schuster, 1959), p. 660.

97. Aristotle, *Politics*, Book I, 1252b.

98. "In the modern world the two realms indeed constantly flow into each other like waves in the never-ending stream of the life-process itself." Arendt, *The Human Condition, op. cit.*, p. 31.

99. Thus, Brzezinski, in speaking of "total social revolution," and Sigmund Neumann, in speaking of "permanent revolution," would seem to have statist totalism in mind.

100. Barrington Moore, Jr., *Political Power, op. cit.*, p. 80. Unfortunately, despite his apparent recognition of the distinction, he makes little use of it in the body of his study.

101. Freedom understood as the absence of *internal* psychological restraints and its relationship to freedom conceived as self-actualization are intelligently examined by Christian Bay in *The Structure of Freedom* (New York: Atheneum, 1965), especially Chaps. 4 and 6. As liberal theorists have long denied the cogency of philosophies positing "positive freedom," some critics of liberal theory are now questioning the meaningfulness of "negative (Lockean) freedom." Herbert Marcuse, for example, charges that "under the rule of a repressive whole, liberty can be made into a powerful instrument of domination. The range of choice open to the individual is not the decisive factor in determining the degree of human freedom, but *what* can be chosen and what *is* chosen by the individual. . . . Free election of masters does not abolish the masters or the slaves. Free choice among a wide variety of goods and services does not signify freedom if these goods and services sustain social controls over a life of toil and fear—that is, if they sustain alienation." *One-Dimensional Man, op. cit.*, pp. 7-8. Such strictures naturally reinforce theories of convergence, in that they suggest that America is as little free as the Soviet Union, although each nation experiences its own peculiar form of unfreedom. In Erich Kahler's portrayal, "The Russian kind of conformism is overtly authoritarian and dogmatically rigid [statist totalism?]; the American kind of conformism is covertly compelling—as by a natural process—and technically flexible [involuntary totalism?]. But conformism it is, here and there. Under both systems a person is forced to sell himself. The Russian way leads to mental enslavement and ideological stultification, the American way leads to all-pervading functionalization and commercialization." *The Tower and the Abyss* (New York: George Braziller, 1957), p. 277.

102. Assuming, indeed, that the Soviet Union *does* approximate such a pattern; in fact, much of the criticism that has been leveled at totalitarianism

as a theory concerns not its conceptual foundations but its appropriateness to the realities of Soviet politics. Michael Curtis' contribution to this volume treats this question thoroughly.

103. See, for example, the indicators provided by such phenomenologically oriented critics of totalitarianism as Carl J. Friedrich, John Kautsky, Karl Deutsch, or R. J. Rummel.

104. Otto Gierke, *Political Theories of the Middle Age* (Boston: Beacon Press, 1958), p. 100.

105. *Ibid.*

106. Tucker, "Movement-Regimes," *op. cit.*, p. 282.

107. The appropriateness of the private-public, egalitarian model even as an explanatory framework for Hobbes or Locke has been under suspicion at least since the appearance of Rousseau's *Discourse on the Origin of Inequality* (which may be one reason why liberals defending the rise of liberal thought have villified Rousseau as a "totalitarian"). C. B. MacPherson also challenges the traditional interpretation in *The Political Theory of Possessive Individualism* (New York: Oxford University Press, 1962), in which many of the problems raised by the attempt to locate and characterize society in the state-of-nature-sovereign state paradigm are explored.

108. The example of the late C. Wright Mills springs immediately to mind, although the undeserved scorn with which he was regarded by many academicians may have been less the result of his radicalism than of his popularity. (If confronted with the choice, it would appear that a number of American scholars would rather see their colleagues Red than read.)

109. The portrait of modern pluralist theory presented here is admittedly something of a caricature; like good caricatures, however, its distortions represent features that are disproportionately prominent in the original subject. A more accurate likeness can be found in David B. Truman's already "classic" modern statement, *The Governmental Process* (New York: Alfred A. Knopf, 1951). The classic classic is, of course, Arthur F. Bentley's *The Process of Government*, first published in 1907 and reissued again in 1967 by the Harvard University Press. An interesting critique from the "Straussian Right" (in contrast to the leftist critiques cited *infra*, N. 112) is Leo Weinstein's "The Group Approach: Arthur F. Bentley," in H. J. Storing (ed.), *Essays on the Scientific Study of Politics* (New York: Holt, Rinehart and Winston, 1962).

110. "In developing a group interpretation of politics, therefore, we do not need to account for a totally inclusive interest, because one does not exist." Truman, *op. cit.*, p. 51. (Shades of the "Invisible Hand"?)

111. Eckstein and Apter, for example, view the totalitarian state as a threat not only to the individual personality, but also to "the groupings of society." Whenever "society" rather than the individual is regarded as the object of totalitarian statist expansion (as, for example, in the definitions of Carl Friedrich, Barrington Moore, Jr., Franz Neumann, *inter alia*), a pluralist orientation can be assumed.

112. For a frankly radical critique of the ideological uses of pluralism by American political scientists, see Shin'ya Ono, "The Limits of Bourgeois Pluralism"; Todd Gitlin, "Local Pluralism as Theory and Ideology"; and Peter

Bachrach and Morton S. Baratz, "Two Faces of Power"; all in Charles A. McCoy and John Playford (eds.), *Apolitical Politics: A Critique of Behavioralism* (New York: Thomas Y. Crowell, 1967).

113. E. E. Schattschneider, *The Semi-Sovereign People* (New York: Holt, Rinehart and Winston, 1960), p. 35.

114. Henry S. Kariel, *The Decline of American Pluralism* (Stanford, Calif.: Stanford University Press, 1961), p. 2.

115. *Ibid.*, p. 4. This leads Peter Bachrach, in his penetrating critique *The Theory of Democratic Elitism* (Boston: Little, Brown, 1967), to suggest that the rehabilitation of democracy under these novel circumstances might require the extension of "participation in decision-making" to large "private" corporations. (See pp. 93-106.)

116. Truman, for example, criticizes "the persistence among nonspecialists of the notion of an inherent conflict between 'the individual' and 'the group' or 'society'" (*op. cit.*, p. 48), but he goes on to say "it is not intended, however, that we should reject the general human values asserted in the militant doctrines of individualism," and seems to concede MacIver's contention that "*laissez-faire* Spencerians, the Marxists, the pluralists, and group interpretations such as Bentley's [are] alike in one respect: 'that they denied or rejected the integrating function of the state.'" (*Ibid.*, p. 50.)

117. This points to a crucial question that space and continuity have not permitted us to deal with here: In addition to the empirical and theoretical problems raised by the concept, totalitarianism incorporates a set of normative assumptions that, although they are not explicitly stated and are apparently taken for granted, are vulnerable to ethical challenges on both prudential and categorical grounds. The value of democratic rulership, limited government, and individualistic, pluralistic social goals, as two thousand years of political theory attests, is anything but self-evident. I hope to be able to give these normative questions the attention they deserve elsewhere.

118. See *Supra*, No. 3.

119. See *Supra*, No. 3.

2.

Retreat from Totalitarianism

MICHAEL CURTIS

Political terminology is a treacherous form of intellectual statement since correct definition of political phenomena is intrinsically difficult and because formulation of policy may depend on that definition. The lack of exact precision with which the phenomena can be analyzed, the problem of positing an explanatory model or method of classification capable of embracing the relevant data, the constant change that imperils the original classification, all suggest caution in the evaluation of political institutions and systems.

Some political terms, nevertheless, are generally acceptable for descriptive purposes. Terms such as executive or monarchy, though their meaning may sometimes be disputed, are relatively neutral in tone. Others, such as freedom, democracy, rights, are more ambiguous, and usually have emotive overtones accompanying any intellectual analysis. The term "totalitarianism" is of the latter nature. Its use has been of significance in both a theoretical and a practical sense. The concept has had an

53

important impact on the way in which Communist systems have been studied and on the reluctance of analysts to bring these systems within the framework of general propositions about comparative politics. Its practical importance derives from the fact that discussion and decision-making of foreign policy may have been influenced by it.

The concept of totalitarianism began to be popularized in the early 1950's. Usage was based on two premises. One was that the similarities between the Communist regime in the Soviet Union and the regimes of Nazi Germany and Fascist Italy were greater than the the differences between them. The second was that the Communist regime was not an ally of, nor did it draw inspiration from, the same sources as the democratic countries but rather must be considered antithetical to the democratic way of life.

The rapid acceptance of the concept may be traced to the sense of impatience in the postwar period at the absence of harmonious international relationships so soon after World War II and to the bewildering complexity of foreign affairs in a world in which new nations were emerging, as well as to the creation of Soviet-dominated Communist systems in Eastern and Central Europe. Paradoxically, the concept coincided with, and was related to, "the end of ideology" thesis, formulated to a considerable degree by those who had become disillusioned by the revelations of political behavior during the Stalinist era. For these writers, of whom Raymond Aron, Daniel Bell, and S. M. Lipset were the most articulate, ideology had ended or become less significant in the Western democracies, while it remained important in the Communist countries.

The concept of totalitarianism has served a valuable and honorable purpose in comparative analysis. But it has also been useful to those believing in the incompatibility of communism and democracy, and to those accepting the inevitability of a cold war with the Soviet Union in particular, or with the Communist countries in general. Internally, within the United States, such a view would tend to restrict the expression of political radicalism. Externally, it has tended to encourage a simplistic response by the United States in international affairs, which have been viewed from the perspective of automatic hostility between the two systems. If Communist countries are automatically viewed as totalitarian, with all the concept's pejorative connotations, they emerge not simply as the inevitable enemy but also as the embodiment of evil and of a heresy to be isolated. In as stark a bipolarity of international relations as this, neutrality would be frowned upon, a potential third force discouraged, and anti-Communist governments supported. National interest would tend to be equated with international equilibrium.

It is true that this view of relationships between East and West can be supported from the Communist canon. The statement of Lenin that "as long as capitalism and socialism exist, we cannot live in peace: in the end, one or the other will triumph" has been echoed on many occasions and has appeared to be an intransigent attitude. Yet, Communist practice has not consistently made this attitude an operative principle of the system.

The danger of acting on the basis of rigid ideological formulas in foreign affairs is readily apparent; the attempt to implement them leads logically to perpetual conflict with, and moral crusades against, the opponents of the formulas. If the ideology is the doctrine of a powerful state, this might then result in the making of an indefinite number of military or other commitments or to continual interference in the affairs of weaker states.

Few in the United States care to take the case for resistance to actions by totalitarian systems to its logical extreme. The argument[1] that it required the theory of totalitarianism to make U.S. postwar foreign policy comprehensible needs serious qualification. American policy has had no consistent ideological motivation of anti-totalitarianism. It has wavered between regarding the Soviet Union as a great power to be treated with caution and as the leader of an international Communist conspiracy. Some American officials, such as John Foster Dulles, may have tended to see foreign policy as an instrument in the Manichean struggle of light against darkness or morality against political evil, but even his Calvinistic view of life was seriously qualified in actual practice and his views on "liberation" and "massive retaliation" were overblown rhetoric. Though George Kennan has altered his point of view from time to time, the containment theory he recommended for American policy in Europe was more concerned with meeting aggressive expansion than with countering an ideological creed.[2] It implied political containment of a political threat, not the containment by military means of a military threat. Moreover, containment was not a policy recommended for application everywhere, but was largely concerned with ensuring that those areas considered vital to American security—Britain, the Rhine Valley and its industry, and Japan—did not come under Communist control. With the death of Stalin, and with the emergence of the Sino-Soviet conflict, the rationale for the policy of containment was itself weakened.

This alternative way of analyzing American policy is a reflection of the inherent ambiguity and complexity of international relations. Ever since the French Revolution and the emergence of modern ideologies that might orient political behavior and affect other nations, relationships among states have been based on a complex compound of ideology and national interest. The relationship between the Soviet Union and the United States has been no exception.

The argument that there is an international Communist conspiracy that is responsible for fomenting all opposition to existing government borders on the paranoic. Few of

allowed one to differentiate the Nazi and Stalinist systems from other forms of contemporary dictatorships and from earlier systems of autocracy or authoritarianism. The term can apply to regimes in which all aspects of political, social, economic, and cultural life are subject to control, no limits to governmental interference are admitted, no political opposition or independent organization is permissible, and all citizens are expected to accept official, infallible doctrine. Even in absolutist regimes such as that of Louis XIV, the power of government was limited by the existence of intermediary institutions and by personal rights such as the right of petition and of association for nonpolitical purposes.[5]

The claims of autocratic government are largely confined to public matters. But in totalitarian systems, the distinction between public and private has largely disappeared, so that official views on matters such as marriage and family life are pronounced. Giovanni Gentile, the major philosophic exponent of fascism, spoke of the totalitarian scope of fascism, which concerned itself not only with political organization and tendency but "with the whole will, thought, and feeling of the nation."[6] For Mussolini (as he stated in his article on fascism in the Italian Encyclopedia), "nothing human or spiritual exists, much less has value, outside the state." Unlike liberalism, which preferred the interest of the individual to the state, fascism would reaffirm the state as the true reality of the individual.

Totalitarian systems are characterized by the elimination of the carefully cultivated distinction made in Western democracies between the state and society, by the absence of restraints on the wielders of power, by strict controls over the dissemination of information, by insistence on the particular truths of the regime, by strong directives over the economy and productive process, by maintaining what Lowenthal has called "a momentum of manipulated change,"[7] by a genuine or purported desire to create a new political and social system, by a single party with dedicated and disciplined adherents, and by a powerful secret police. Total power was explained from the premises of the regime: in Stalinist Russia, the dictatorship of the proletariat required the heightening of state power; in Germany, Hitler used the themes of the *Volk* and the organic community to explain Nazi concern for the whole; and in Italy, Mussolini thought the power of the state coextensive with the whole community.

Many of these characteristics have been present in earlier systems: in ancient and medieval despotisms, the Anabaptist regime in Munster, the Spanish evangelizing of Mexico in the sixteenth century, the Inca empire, Calvin's Geneva, nineteenth-century autocracies. But two new factors are present in contemporary systems: a highly technological society, which allows both an increase in the range and scope of control over citizens and a reduction in inefficiency, and an appeal by rulers to the mass of citizenry for support. The control inherent in the use of modern technology constitutes a danger for democratic as well as nondemocratic regimes, and the dependence of developed societies on computers has brought the fear that decisions in future may be taken by those controlling the operation of the computers rather than by elected representatives.

Some commentators have found in the latter factor—the fact that contemporary societies are mass societies—the key to totalitarian movements that try to weld estranged individuals into a community. Hannah Arendt views totalitarianism as arising out of the atomization of alienated and anxious individuals in modern society where the old foundations of the political realm, religion, tradition, and authority, are weak and in need of repair.[8] In Kornhauser's mass society, nonelites are readily available for mobilization by elites. Lasswell has seen totalitarianism as providing an outlet for aggressive tendencies that can be directed against either subgroups within the society or foreigners. For Cantril, totalitarianism illustrates the psychology of mass despair and the lack of attachment to community that opens the door to a leadership promising direction and unity. For Talmon, totalitarian democracy, resting on popular enthusiasm, results from the pursuit of a preordained harmonious and perfect scheme of things to which men are irresistably drawn.[9]

It is this insistence on mass participation or enthusiasm that differentiates totalitarianism from other similar non-democratic regimes. An authoritarian regime such as Spain under Franco is conservative in outlook, closely tied to Catholicism and to monarchists, supported by the army, capable of imposing strong economic controls, but it is equally ready to make any necessary compromise with the social forces in the country and does not seek out mass support.[10] Indeed, the hopes of the Falangists to use a syndicalist party to attract workers were ended by Franco in April, 1937, when he created a unified movement of traditionalists and Falangists under his own control and imprisoned the Falangist leader Manuel Hedilla, who had refused to become his assistant in the new movement.[11] A prospective radical group appealing to the masses was transformed into a political machine concerned with patronage.

In the first years of his dictatorship, Franco called the regime *totalitario*, but this was essentially a "synonym for *organico*" (organized)[12] rather than a state patterned on the Italian model. Political assembly is still illegal without official permission, no public criticism of the key political leaders is allowed, censorship and a secret police are in existence, but some free expression is tolerated and works by democratic socialist writers are available in the bookstores. Portugal, both under Salazar and under his successor, Marcello Caetano, has a censored press, rigged elections, a secret political police, a single legal party, and according to its self-image, a civilizing mission abroad, but, because of its traditional and reactionary nature, it can be regarded as an example of "clerical conservatism"[13] rather than of totalitarianism.

To gain sufficient strength to obtain power, the Italian Fascist and German Nazi regimes sought support from parts of the capitalist and aristocratic classes, military officers, and higher clergy, but they were never dominated by, or submissive to, the interests of these groups as the clerical conservative regimes have been. Nor do these latter regimes claim the certitude on political and ethical matters possessed by totalitarian systems. If authoritarian regimes and traditional authorities provide mutual support, totalitarian systems see themselves as the creators of secular standards and values without dependence on religious ethics. The former systems are not prone to dominate social behavior, groups, and institutions, to employ as great a degree of ruthlessness, to forbid freedom outside the political realm, to ignore legal procedure, compel acceptance of official doctrine, or neglect traditional values to the same extent as the latter regimes.

In similar fashion, the newer systems owe little to past theorists. In an age of universal suffrage and appeals to the people, the creation of movements that would be both the means of capturing political power and the source of such power was accompanied by new doctrines, myths, and symbolic references. The list of supposed intellectual precursors of totalitarianism is long but must be treated with great caution. While some of the ideas or general orientation of writers such as Plato, Machiavelli, the French Enlightenment authors, Rousseau, Fichte, Hegel, Saint-Simon, Comte, Treitschke, and Nietzsche can be juxtaposed alongside the themes of nazism or communism, this does not mean that the core of their views is harmonious with that of the totalitarian systems.[14]

The most influential analysis of totalitarianism has been that provided by Friedrich and Brzezinski,[15] who argue that all totalitarian dictatorships possess six common traits: an official ideology, a single party usually with a dominant leader, a secret police and the use of terror, a monopoly of communications, a monopoly of weapons, and a centrally directed economy. In his present contribution to this book, Carl Friedrich, attempting to cope with recent changes in the Communist world, has amended his definition to embrace a regime that has a totalist official ideology, a party whose authority is reinforced by a secret police, and a monopoly control over mass communications, operational weapons, and all organizations, including economic activities.

Useful as the concept of totalitarianism has been as an explanatory tool for distinguishing political systems, reservations of two kinds are in order. The first is that the concept is only partly applicable to the three countries—Germany, the Soviet Union, and, especially, Italy—out of whose experience the theory was erected, and this has great importance in properly evaluating these countries. The second is that political behavior in the Soviet Union has changed sufficiently to render the concept inadequate. Moreover, the polycentrism of the Communist countries makes a monolithic explanation incorrect.

IDEOLOGY AND POWER

The first characteristic of Friedrich's definition of totalitarianism is an official ideology as an "action-related system of ideas." Despite varying degrees of intellectual support from individuals such as Martin Heidegger, Carl Schmitt, and Gentile, the ragbag of ideas or myths on which political action purportedly rested in the Italian Fascist and German Nazi regimes can hardly be regarded as an ideological system or be deemed worthy of intellectual respectability. Gentile himself wrote that fascism was not a philosophy, it was not "even a political theory which may be stated in a series of formulae." The Italian corporative system smacked of charlatanism. The Italian historian Gaetano Salvemini was only one of many who saw the corporative concept as elaborate and imposing humbug.[16] The twenty-two separate categories for the different trades and industries were more useful in providing jobs for party officials and in controlling labor and possible strikes than in providing an oversight of the economy. Though fascism proclaimed itself as both anti-Communist and anticapitalist, it had initially no economic policy and, in fact, allowed private capitalism to continue. Only later, with imposition of some controls over credit, allocation of materials and labor, prices and profits, licensing and rationing, did some central planning come into effect.

The socialism and syndicalism of Mussolini's early career, the concept of man as producer (rather than as citizen) existing most appropriately in a corporativist system, was largely forgotten during his tenure of power; it reappeared only in defeat when, retrenched in the "Salo Republic" (1943-45) and propped up by the Germans, Mussolini stressed the need "to return to the origins." Far more important and crucial in Fascist doctrine were the themes of creating a new era in history, the new Rome—"The Rome of the Blackshirts, at once ancient and modern"—building a strong, disciplined state, and offering obedience to Il Duce, infallible leader and founder of the regime. At best, fascism can be said to be an inchoate response to a fear of the coming decline of modern civilization. What is vital in it are those qualities most appropriate to earlier eras: action, duty, discipline, bravery, loyalty, self-denial. Like nazism, though less deliberately, it was an appeal to the spirit of the brotherhood of the trenches of World War I.

In Germany, the major themes of Nazism were equally lacking in intellectual content. The original twenty-five

points of the 1920 Nazi program were disregarded by
Hitler, who also ignored the work of Alfred Rosenberg,
the major ideologue of the movement. Although the writer
Charles Maurras, the French counterrevolutionary, once
argued that "a socialism that has been freed of democratic
and cosmopolitan elements can fit nationalism like a
well-made glove fits a beautiful hand,"[17] the socialist
elements of National Socialism disappeared both intellec-
tually and physically as the Strassers and others who held
them were liquidated. Racialism not rational thought was
at the core of nazism. Hitler's views on the supremacy of
the Aryan race, life as a struggle, man as brutal, pan-Ger-
manism, violent anti-Semitism, complete obedience to the
leader, made up a crude kind of Social Darwinism.[18]
Indeed, Herbert Luethy has written of Hitler's sick,
obscene savagery, his depraved fantasies, which were
elevated into the official philosophy of a civilized nation.[19]
Without Hitler, there were no Nazi ideas, and he had no
real economic or political program apart from anti-Semitism, the creation of national unity, and expansion to the
east. There was no projection of the future in any sense
other than the inculcation of military values, acquisition of
land, or maintenance of racial purity. The Nazi regime, like
the Italian, was little more than a preparation for war.
Hitler's declaration of a policy of force, made on November 5, 1937, and the secret admission that his objective
was *Lebensraum* to the east seem to provide the key to the
nature of the regime. Unlike the Communist preoccupation
with planning in economic and social matters, the German
four-year plans were primarily concerned with military
matters and with making Germany economically self-sufficient.

In his *Memoirs*, Alfred Rosenberg spoke of the regime as
a "theatrocracy" in which the artistic side of Hitler's
character overwhelmed him in a paroxysm of self-intoxica-
tion. To this can be attributed the spectacular extrava-
ganzas, the deliberate production of organized excitement,

the torchlight processions, the emotional rhetoric and demagoguery of the regime. Far from being based on elaborate analysis or ideological orientation, much of Hitler's action resulted from improvisation, shrewd intuition, fanatical determination, histrionic plausability, and a skillful use of potential allies. Even the Reichstag fire, which proved to be the work of a demented Dutch socialist acting alone, allowed Hitler to consolidate his power, providing him with "a heaven-sent opportunity" to end political opposition.[20] The Nazi revolution was, as Rauschning wrote, a revolution without a doctrine.[21]

For the Communist party in Russia, ideology has been crucial ever since Lenin, in *What is to be Done?*, declared that without revolutionary theory there could be no revolutionary movement. In Lenin's view, both then and later, the connection between consciousness and revolutionary practice was close. The revolution could succeed only if the proletariat developed its own consciousness and devotion to the revolution, and this would be accomplished by ideological understanding.

The term "ideology" has always been tinged with ambiguity. A term used by Marx to criticize the preoccupation with ideas rather than with real social and economic phenomena, it now refers to the interrelated beliefs held by a person, group, or regime, which can provide a total vision of man and the world. Moreover, it suggests a purposefulness and a general orientation of doctrine the impact of which is comparable with religious faith or scientific truth. It was against this purposefulness of ideology that Abram Tertz (Sinyavsky) wrote, in his essay on socialist realism: "I put my hope in a phantasmagoric art, with hypotheses instead of a Purpose." [22] The mixture of reason and myth that makes up a totalitarian ideology is accepted or imposed on the members of a regime on the basis that this official doctrine is the unique truth. Official ideology becomes dogma, accepted uncritically. Rulers demand from their subjects not silence, as in autocratic regimes, but hymns of praise. At the same time, "ideology" has also been taken to mean the intellectual process by which political positions, actions, and nonactions are justified or rationalized. It thus constitutes the rationale for the interest of those formulating the ideology. The essential role of ideology thus becomes the preservation of the existing social order, as Karl Mannheim suggested,[23] or, even more realistically, the mask for the exercise of power.

Ideology in the Soviet Union—the Marxist-Leninist and, formerly, Stalinist views on political, economic, and social matters—has been erected into a majestic intellectual structure, the scope of which has embraced the whole political culture of the community. The interrelated logic of its constituent parts has appealed to those wanting emotional assurance in an uncertain world as well as to those accepting the rationality of its argument. But analysts differ sharply on the significance and relevance of ideology in the Soviet Union, and on its relationship to political action. Views range from those of Hans Morgenthau, who argues that ideology essentially masks the contest for power or makes it psychologically and morally acceptable to the actors and their audience, to those of Nathan Leites, who believes that Soviet behavior can be understood or deduced from the Marxist literature. Czeslaw Milosz has seen Soviet ideology both as the self-legitimizer of the rulers and of the Communist party and as a method by which to check criticism or doubt. Alfred Meyer and others have viewed it as a public relations device, a process through which reality can be distorted or concealed.

The enigma remains as to whether ideology in the Soviet Union has been a guide to action, in Stalin's phrase, or a rationalization of it. Is it the rationale for the maintenance or increase of the power of the rulers in internal and external affairs or the intellectual mainstream of Soviet thought? Does ideology truly motivate the actions of the rulers or is it simply, as Meyer has said, the code of communication in the Soviet Union, the medium of public discourse, the language of politics? Is ideology now internalized and ritualized, as Carl Friedrich has suggested, or is it a language that is not always taken seriously? Is ideology useful for political understanding or prediction, or is it a bizarre ritual comparable, as Trevor-Roper suggested, to Byzantine theology or to the big end-little end egg dispute in Lilliput.[24]

Clearly, ideology in the Soviet Union has influenced policy-making to some degree. This largely explains the greater emphasis on the sovkhozy (state farms) rather than the kolkhozy (collective farms), since the former have not been regarded as more productive bodies, the desire to end the distinction between collective peasants and state workers, the stress on collective farms rather than private agricultural plots (though the output of the latter is potentially greater), the creation of large farms, and the location of machine-tractor stations. The economic structure, agricultural communal organizations, attitudes to material incentives and piece rates, the restricted use of rent, advertising, flexible prices, and consumer credit can largely be attributed to ideological impact.[25] Communist ideology reinforced the excesses of war communism, the actions against private farming, and the refusal of Stalin to consider alternative policies to the liquidation of the kulaks.[26] In external affairs, the ideological framework of irreconcilable antagonism between communism and capitalism helped create and perpetuate that very antagonism and led Soviet leaders to hold preconceived views of the international scene.[27]

In reality, Soviet ideology has been a flexible rather than a consistent body of doctrine. Ideas have been altered or interpretations changed where necessary to take account of political, social, and economic developments, to respond to the needs of industrialization and aid the growth of heavy industry. The decline in ideological rigidity began with Lenin's realization that the anticipated revolution in the West would not be immediately forthcoming and that internal conditions required a New Economic Policy; it has continued since then as existing doctrine was found to be inapplicable to changing needs. Correspondingly, there has been a decline in ideological intensity as foreign policy has changed.

Under Stalin, ideology became readily adaptable to embrace his advocacy of "socialism in one country," forced collectivization, the heightened role of the state, the conception of nonantagonistic classes, the emphasis on the nation and on patriotism rather than on class. Ideology was manipulated by the ruler to lend greater legitimacy to his acts. The theory of "socialism in one country" provided a rationale for the attacks on Trotsky and others; the concept of "capitalist encirclement of the Soviet Union" justified ruthless repression within the country; the view of "Titoist revisionism" helped defend tighter Soviet control over the satellite countries. The very flexibility of Stalin's positions and his arbitrary changes suggest the absence of any integrated doctrine during his rule. Adherence to Marxism-Leninism-Stalinism lent plausibility to demands on workers for greater effort, a policy of heightened chauvinism, and the consolidation of the power of the ruler.

Doubt has often been cast on the relevance of Marxist theory to Communist practice. In science, the controversy over Lysenko and genetics showed the relevance was not self-evident. Stalin's intervention in the field of linguistics and his view that language, though part of the superstructure, is independent of social conditions contradicted a basic concept of Marxist philosophy.[28] Marxist economic theory has contributed little to the solution of production or organizational problems or the use of economic resources. Many have seen the decisive factor in the history of Soviet economic policy as economic underdevelopment rather than Marxism.[29]

It is plain that the appeal of communism is often the result of admiration for the success of Soviet industrialization rather than ideological identification. The Soviet Union built industry rather than socialism, concerned itself with its own security and material interests more than with the interests of the world proletariat or the destiny of other communist countries. Stalin, in *The Problems of Leninism*, deliberately appealed to national pride and material interests: "Do you want our socialist fatherland to be beaten and lose its independence? [If not] you must put an end to its backwardness in the shortest possible time." Messianic salvation was equated with the needs of the Russian state.

Part of the general problem in discussing the meaningfulness of Communist ideology stems from the disputed inheritance of Marxism. Correct interpretation of the Marxist liturgy has, since the days of Marx and Engels themselves, been a matter of intellectual speculation, and the value of the Leninist version is not synonymous with his successful revolutionary tactics. The theoretical difficulty has been compounded by two practical problems: the Sino-Soviet dispute and the polycentrism of the Communist movement.

Differences in ideological expostulation between the Soviet Union and China stem from the dissimilar revolutionary experiences of the two countries as well as from their varied historical backgrounds. The Russian Bolsheviks unexpectedly captured power and then extended the degree and range of state authority. The Chinese Communists had, over a twenty-year process, been building an embryonic political and military authority. Early attempts at centralization of the Chinese system gave way to greater autonomy at the local level and to the increased use of work teams and brigades and basic party units.[30] Chinese underdevelopment has meant a reliance on the mobilization of vast numbers for construction work simultaneously in heavy and light industry and in agriculture. But it has also meant the formulation of the theory that the major areas of mutual antagonism are no longer the capitalist countries among whom war is inevitable through industrial rivalry but between the industrialized and the developing countries. The latter countries, rather than the highly industrialized countries of original Marxist analysis, thus become the area of global contradictions and the center of the world revolution, if only as participants in the struggle against American imperialism.

Maoism presents itself as the theory for essentially peasant, underdeveloped societies as contrasted with the Soviet doctrine, which is no longer concerned primarily with revolutionary exhortation. But the ideological differences between China and the Soviet doctrine are compounded by, and indeed may be the rationalization of, the natural hostility of two great powers claiming domination of, or seeking to influence, a world-wide movement, of old boundary disputes between the two countries, which go back to the beginning of the century, of the problem of the Khazak minority in Sinkiang and the settlements on frontier lands by both countries.

Soviet control over all Communist movements has given way to polycentrism. International communism has become the conflict of national communisms in each of which ideology reflects national interests and different historical and cultural experiences. Some doctrines have taken on democratic overtones, as in Togliatti's "Italian Way to Socialism" where the goal could not be reached "outside the fabric of Italian democratic life." There is no longer any necessary coherent relationship between ideology in external and internal matters, as is illustrated by Rumania, whose manifestation of independence from the

Soviet Union in foreign policy has not led it to liberalize its regime. Rivalries between the Communist countries over disputed territory, as between Poland and East Germany, or between Bulgaria and Yugoslavia over Macedonia, make mockery of the theoretical international solidarity of the Communist world. In view of all these factors, it is difficult to see how ideology in the Communist world can possess any particular doctrinal content shared in common.

Related to the stress on ideology as a characteristic of totalitarianism is the view that the purpose of totalitarian regimes is, as Brzezinski put it, "effecting a total social revolution, including the conditioning of man." It is true that, in Germany, Rosenberg argued that the task of our century was "to create a new human type out of a new life myth," and that Hitler, at the 1937 Nazi party congress, said German racial policy was creating the new man. But the definition of the new German type, as he indicated on another occasion, was an individual slim and lithe, fast as a greyhound, tough as leather, and hard as Krupp steel. The 8 million members of Hitler Youth trained in sports and military discipline from the age of six to eighteen and spent six months compulsory service on the land. The purpose was made clear by Hitler in May, 1936: "We must ask for a hard youth, so that one day, when life comes upon youth in all its hardness, it may not surrender or grow weak." From the fact that Hitler exterminated whole parts of the German community, it does not follow that either nazism or fascism was dedicated to any real social or human transformation. The *homo fascista*—a virile, forceful, energetic, creative creature capable of action and will—was as much a figure of myth as Mussolini himself.

It is only in Marxist theory that the concept of individual transformation through social change can be sustained; yet, it is doubtful whether this objective is now eagerly sought by the Soviet Union or by the Eastern

European countries. Only in China has there been a consistent attempt to change human behavior and transform particularist loyalties to the family, class, or village into loyalty to the country or the party. Chinese attempts to control behavior have embraced a variety of methods; control over communication, thought reform, personal manipulation, confession, self-criticism, group study, debasement of language, public denunciation, and people's control correspondents who were known to be informers.[31] In recent years, the attempt to control behavior has been illustrated in extraordinary fashion by the Cultural Revolution, aimed at the transformation of social relationships and at the undermining of those entrenched in power in the party and the state.

The austerity of the Chinese revolutionaries, their deep moral conviction, their constant reiteration and devotion to the texts of the master, Mao, exemplify not only a modern form of religious moralism, but also both the eagerness of an underdeveloped country to strengthen itself and the continuity with the Chinese past. Much of the present behavior resembles the old Chinese methods of censorship, the Confucian ideas of orthodoxy, loyalty, and the rectification of names. Yet, the constant activity and frenzied behavior of youthful extremists and Red Guards shows the very lack of success of the attempt at indoctrination and the remaking of man. In particular, the communes that were supposed to replace family loyalty, pool property, organize work, impose military discipline, make communal eating arrangements, and liberate women have not become "the most beautiful flower of Marxism" that the Chinese leaders envisaged.

Paradoxically, the Cultural Revolution—like the Great Leap Forward of ten years earlier, which tried to combine industry, agriculture, and education within the framework of the commune—has been uneconomic and inefficient. Ideological rampages have slowed down the movement to economic modernization. Old disputes between clans and villages have reoccurred, and the campaign to create a new revolutionary spirit has helped make such a spirit more improbable.

An argument of the theorists of totalitarianism has been that expansionism is a feature common to totalitarian systems. It is true that the three countries all found convenient enemies on whom hatred could be focused in both mythological and practical fashion, and that "race" in one case, "the glory that was Rome" in the second, and "world communism" in the third might be used to justify expansion. Yet, if Germany and Italy were given to territorial aggrandizement, this was not so much a logical consequence of their doctrines as the result of the past history of the two countries and of their internal problems. The Nazi and Fascist regimes were marked by their bellicose nature, their heightened nationalism, their emotional fervor, their opportunistic adventurism.

In the Soviet Union, even during the Stalinist period, the regime was more isolationist than expansionist, and its acquisition of territory was dictated more by reason of supposed military security than by logical theory. The lack of relationship between communism and an expansionist policy is clearly evident in the case of the Balkan states. They are no more aggressive under Communist rule than they were in pre-World War II Europe when some of these regimes were virtually Fascist in character. Aggressiveness would appear to be the outcome of the size and power of the state rather than of any propelling ideas of the regime.

THE DICTATOR AND TERROR

A second major feature of the concept of totalitarianism is the key role of terror in all three regimes. Indeed, much of the popularity of the original argument for the concept rested, overtly or implicitly, on the place of terror or the role of the secret police, so that the symbol of a totalitarian system became the concentration camp. Arendt, Brzezinski, and Fainsod each argued in similar fashion. Fainsod, for example, in the 1953 edition of his book *How Russia is Ruled*, said that "terror is the linchpin of modern totalitarianism . . . [together with a secret police] it forms an organized system of power." But the theorists have been obliged to qualify their argument for two reasons: the knowledge of the complete ascendancy of the leader in the regimes, and the reduction of the place of terror in the Soviet Union in recent years.

The character of the rulers has been of crucial significance in the shaping of the regimes. The Soviet Union, by admission of its own contemporary leaders, has been peculiarly unfortunate since, for thirty years, it was ruled by traitors and by a paranoic mass-murderer, and, for ten years, by incompetents or harebrained schemers. In the three regimes, power was personalized. A law enacted in January, 1926 gave Mussolini power to issue decrees, and some 100,000 were issued during the Fascist regime, though not all were formulated by Il Duce himself. In the Soviet Union, Stalin as the Vozhd', the supreme leader, dominated the whole political process. In Germany, the Enabling Act of March, 1933 allowed Hitler, as Chancellor, to make laws for four years without having to gain the permission of the Reichstag, and the Reich cabinet never met after 1937.

To a very large degree, terror in the Soviet Union and in Germany resulted from the idiosyncratic views and temperamental abnormality of the dictator, sometimes affected by the historical tradition and culture of the country. All nondemocratic regimes have imposed controls over free expression, many have made use of a secret police, and some have incarcerated political prisoners. But, where the personal paranoia of a dictator is not present—as with Salazar, an austere, reserved economist who was

utterly lacking in flamboyance and uninterested in cere-
mony, or with Franco, a conservative military officer and
traditionalist—terror has been of much less significance or
has been applied for specific and comprehensible, if
abhorrent, reasons. This is true even for Mussolini, a
sensual and cynical adventurer, an empty showman with a
gift for publicizing himself, a clown pretending to be
Superman, whose major innovation in politics was the use
of castor oil.[32]

Hitler, the self-confessed fanatical anti-Semite, argued in
Mein Kampf that "the supreme art of all really great folk
leaders has always consisted above all in not dividing the
attention of the people but in constantly concentrating it
against one enemy." Hatred, fear, terror were all linked
together against the agents of plutocratic Judaeo-Bolshev-
ism. With his remarkable charismatic appeal, Hitler cultivated his willpower: "My whole life," he said, "can be
summed up as the ceaseless effort to persuade other
people." Franz Von Papen was not alone in speaking of
Hitler's extraordinary capacity for binding individuals and
the masses to his will.[33] And this capacity included
ruthlessness. The state, Hitler argued, "can be maintained
only by a rule of iron: take away the laws, and the fabric
falls immediately to pieces."

The German collective will was supposed to be a
political reality which found its expression in the Führer,
whose authority existed for, and found its justification in,
the people. "The German people," said Hitler, "has elected
a single deputy as its representative with 38 million
votes ... I feel myself just as responsible to the German
people as would any parliament." But Hitler also spoke of
the enormous power of the great masses to forget, and of
the greatness of every mighty organization in intolerantly
imposing its will against all others. His dictatorship was
concerned, above all, with the extension of his own power
and that of Germany by all possible means.

Revolutions in the past have frequently led to terror; in his later writings, Trotsky often alluded to the Soviet regime by analogy with the French Revolution. But, in fact, the Russian Revolution did not follow the pattern of the French in the reaction against extremism. Greater terror rather than a Thermidorian Reaction was the work of the Stalinist era, and the dictator retained power and controlled the party rather than losing it to the army, as in previous dictatorships.

Terror in Russia was no new phenomenon, used by either defenders or opponents of the regime. The roots of Bolshevism lie in Russian history, culture, and religion.[34] The lack of familiarity with freedom in Russia, as well as the economic backwardness of the country and its eagerness to implement communist doctrine, help explain extremist behavior. The Oprichnina was important as early as the reign of Ivan IV. On the other side, arguments for violence and terror were inspired by Chernyshevsky, the nineteenth-century writer and prototype of the revolutionary hero, and by the Russian Populists, such as Tkachev, who thought that a revolutionary movement of disciplined conspirators was the best method to fight Czarist tyranny.[35] Herzen prophetically spoke of the day "when Genghis Khan will return with the telegraph." This anticipation of despotic rule was borne out with the Leninist conception of party—a group of professional conspirators with no private lives of their own, obeying discipline, imposing a revolution from above with ruthless compulsion. The party would become the instrument for the dictatorship of the proletariat.

Nevertheless, there was no functional need for terror in the Soviet Union after civil war had ended and foreign troops had been repulsed. Objective explanations[36] for the historical use of terror—the pressure of foreign or civil wars, an acute economic crisis, the pursuit of a religious faith, internal power struggles—were irrelevant to the

Soviet situation. Indeed, the terror was dysfunctional since it led to widespread famine and the slaughter of millions as well as to the extermination of capable leaders and executives in all fields. Talmon's thesis of totalitarian democracy[37] attempting to impose certitude in politics is based on the dubious premise that genuine convictions and ideas were to be implemented. The labor camps, death ships, resettlement of whole peoples, and Draconian laws on property hardly bear out this thesis. More important is his argument that those who come to power were "not the philosophers with a clear knowledge of the truth but the most arrogant power seekers, the most insolent tyrants."[38]

Recent studies have shown that the casualties under Stalin "were too great for any attainable political or social objective."[39] During the purges, 1 million were executed, at least 12 million died in the labor camps between 1936 and 1950; probably 20 million were killed during all the years of Stalin's rule. Within the Communist party itself, less than 2 per cent of the delegates at the 1934 party congress reappeared at the 1939 congress. In the Central Committee of the party, 55 of the 71 full members were eliminated. Between 1936 and 1939, half of the 2.5 million members of the party were arrested, and only 50,000 regained freedom. Almost every regimental commander in the Soviet army was purged. The humiliating and ruthless manner in which the arrested were obliged to confess to imaginary crimes, plots, and sabotage in show trials fully bore out Rosa Luxemburg's prediction that without free expression in Russia there would come "a brutalization of public life." The classic explanations offered by Koestler's character Gletkin in *Darkness at Noon* for the objective need of terror (in order to safeguard the revolution against world reaction) and for the acceptance by the victim of his undeserved fate (because of his dedication to the principles of the revolution) are inadequate in the light of the methods of extortion, threats to the family as well as to the individual himself, and irrational violence.

The personal nature of the terror in the Soviet Union is illustrated by three factors. The first is that hardly a single distinguished individual in the party, the state organs, the military, the professions, or even in the secret police itself, survived the terror. No one but Stalin understood the point, if there was one, of the ceaseless killings. Moreover, the terror increased in 1934, when any possible internal political opposition or criticism had ended, rather than in 1928, when Stalin had not fully consolidated his power base.[40] After the murder of Kirov on December 1, 1934 (probably at the instigation of Stalin himself), faithful Stalinists like Kuibyshev, Ordzhonikidze, and Rudzutak were all eliminated. Throughout the Purge, the NKVD played the role of agent of terror, the same role the SS played under Hitler. And, with the death of Stalin, the terror has virtually ended, and the power of the secret police has been drastically reduced.

Stalin's cynicism or paranoia becomes apparent when one reads that he warned of "the mortal dangers to the party of the method of amputation and bloodletting." It was Stalin who, in the first issue of *Pravda*, wrote that "we think that a strong and vigorous movement is inconceivable without controversy. A total conformity of opinion can only lead to the cemetery."[41]

Stalin's paradoxical explanation, in March, 1937, for the existence of "the wreckers, murderers, and foreign agents" he had found in all organizations and at all levels was that the greater the successes of socialism, the sharper would be the class struggle inside the country. This explanation was rightly rejected by Khrushchev in 1956. A similar view was propounded by Mao in 1949: "After the enemies with guns have been wiped out, there will still be enemies without guns . . . [and] we must never regard these enemies lightly." In his 1957 speech "On the Correct

Handling of Contradictions Among the People," Mao again argued that "even when all the counter-revolutionaries in existence have been rooted out, new ones may emerge."[42] Yet, despite all the turmoil in China and the reverence for Mao as great teacher, great supreme commander, and great helmsman of the country, Mao has treated those regarded as political opponents far more leniently than did Stalin.

Those who formulated the theory of totalitarianism have tended to regard the characteristic features of totalitarianism as inherent in a Communist system no matter who holds power. But the nature of the Soviet Union was, under Stalin, quite different from what it was under his predecessor and his successors. Stalin, the man close to the Russian demimonde and probably a Czarist agent in his early career, was the key figure in the increase and decrease of terror at will and the individual in whom power was concentrated. Political legitimacy was located in the office of the secretary-general of the Communist party. Power was exercised by the dictator through chosen instruments such as the secret police, the Central Control Commission, and the State Control Commission as well as through the party, government, and military hierarchy. Unclear jurisdictional lines, overlapping of personnel, lack of clear responsibility of officials—all strengthened Stalin's position. The role played by Stalin was similar to that of Hitler, who had remarked that he "was responsible for the fate of the German people. . . . [and had] become the Supreme Justiciar of the German people," even should this mean acting in opposition to the party, the army, the administration, and the cabinet. For both Stalin and Hitler, with their intense lust for power, world history was the result of the activity of single individuals.

Stalin was the center of the Soviet political universe. Boris Nikolaevsky's Old Bolshevik (Bukharin) said, in 1933, that "everyone emphasized tirelessly his devotion to Stalin. It was rather a fight for influence over Stalin, a fight for his soul."[43] Khrushchev talked of his capricious and despotic character. Abram Tertz saw him as mysterious, omniscient, all-powerful—the living monument of the era.

Surely, if the concept of totalitarianism applies to the Soviet Union at all, it is relevant only to the Stalinist regime, with its denial of any moral or spiritual authority independent of the will of Stalin and with its emphasis on conspiracy. As Sidney Hook has argued, it was Stalin, not communism, that condemned abstract art and music.[44] None of Stalin's successors can be regarded as serious theoreticians—or even as minor epigoni in the cast of disciples of Marx—with any claim to embody or define the true faith. The political leader is no longer the chief ideologue, as in the case of Lenin and Stalin. Nor can those in the line of succession from Stalin—what Bertram Wolfe has called "the law of diminishing dictators"—be regarded as the fount of political legitimacy.

Much of the original argument for the acceptance of the concept of totalitarianism rested, by implication, on the large role of terror in the regime, the prominence of the secret police, and the impossibility of resistance. Terror was regarded as the vital nerve of the totalitarian system; for Brzezinski, it was the most universal characteristic of totalitarianism. The reduction, if not elimination, in the role of terror and the secret police, therefore logically suggests a change has occurred in the nature of the Soviet regime, which thus merits a new description.

The analysts of totalitarianism have amended their views. Ten years after his original formulation, Fainsod argued that "every totalitarian regime makes some place for terror in its system of controls ... an awareness of its potentialities conditions the behavior of the totalitarian subject."[45] The Khrushchev era was thus seen as "rationalized" or "enlightened" totalitarianism, which modified the worst grievances of the Stalinist epoch. In a similar vein,

Brzezinski has suggested that terror must be regarded as the product of a particular stage in the development of the Soviet system, the "breakthrough" stage of totalitarianism, and that indoctrination, the particular function of ideologues, has become a more distinctive feature of Soviet life.[46]

Friedrich also has suggested that "terror and secret police cannot be taken by themselves as the decisive trait of totalitarian rule," and he has argued that physical terror has been replaced by psychic terror and the deliberate creation of consensus through the manipulation of mass communications. In contemporary jargon, such a regime is the most modern form of political socialization and political communication is penetrative.[47]

The significance of the process of indoctrination is undeniable, as is indicated by the figure of 36 million people attending adult education courses in the Soviet Union in 1964, though it has not yet reached a situation similar to that in Cuba in which youngsters are kept in their schools from the ages of eight to eighteen, seeing their parents only once a month. In many ways, the Communist countries have sought to reach that state described by Swift, in talking about the Houyhnhnms, where "reason is not a point problematical . . . but strikes you with immediate conviction: as it must needs do, where it is not mingled, obscured or discolored by Passion and Interest." Indoctrination through ideology prevents thought: "What is not expressed," Milosz wrote, "does not exist."[48] In China, brainwashing and doctrinal rigidity, from the beginning of the regime to the Thought Propaganda Teams of 1968, which disseminate the thoughts of Mao, are even more pernicious than in the Soviet Union.

Yet, the process of indoctrination, stifling though it is, is of a quite different order from the terror and the concentration camps of the Stalin and Hitler regimes. It is different from a situation in which the executive branch might be the police rather than the party or state, or in which the SS, devoid of ideological belief except loyalty to the Führer, at times dominated politics. Indeed, it is so different that analysis of the current Soviet regime requires a different formulation and classification.

A logical consequence of totalitarian terror is the difficulty of resisting the regime. Arendt has argued in several places[49] that obedience and support are the same in politics, and that people in a totalitarian country are trapped in universal complicity. In Italy, Mussolini might have been brought down after the murder of Matteotti in 1924 had his opponents not taken to the Aventine, but his power did not end until his regime was in crisis; the Fascist Grand Council voted against him for the first time in July, 1943.

In Germany, opponents of the Nazi regime were not lacking, but all attempts at resistance failed. Army figures like Beck and Witzleben, ecclesiastics like Faulhaber and Niemöller, students like those in the Munich White Rose in 1943, aristocrats like the Kreisau Circle grouped around Moltke, all were cautious resisters. But the July 20, 1944 attempt by Count von Stauffenberg indicated that only assassination of Hitler could change the political regime.

Public political opposition to the Soviet regime virtually ended with the 1921 banning of factionalism and the dissolution of all alternative groups. Stalin's terror eliminated the possibility of any conspiracy; since his death, one unsuccessful attempt, in 1957, to depose Khrushchev, as well as the later successful one in 1964, and the demonstrations in East Germany in 1953, in Hungary in 1956, and in Czechoslovakia in 1968, have shown that opposition to official policy could be registered, even if there were no legal opposition as in Western democracies.

A second argument related to the use of terror in the Soviet Union may also be questioned. A currently fashionable view, held, in different ways, by Meyer, Organski,

Rostow, Deutscher, Brzezinski, and others[50] has seemed to imply a kind of inevitability about the historical process in that the early formative period of a society with its need for primitive accumulation of the means of production requires austerity and restraint on the part of the citizenry and strong, possibly despotic or totalitarian government. The obverse of this view is that the chief aim of communism is the promotion of industrialization in economically underdeveloped societies. The implication is that, to become modernized, nations might have to accept terror, the elimination of groups and traditions, large work assignments, scant material rewards, expendable human beings.

There is, however, no certainty, or "ineluctable drift" as Coser calls it,[51] about the nature of modernizing societies. The view that totalitarianism is a by-product of rapid industrialization in the Soviet Union is rightly rejected by Aron, who holds that "to reduce totalitarianism to the means or the adjunct of industrial society" is to misunderstand historical fact.[52] Such a view also has limited value for comparative analysis since the Nazi regime occurred in an already highly modernized economy.

The argument that a one-party, if not totalitarian, system is necessary for economic modernization, political development, or nation-building, though often made (especially by African leaders) is, in many ways, a specious one. Single-party regimes are not necessarily better agents of economic change than are other regimes, nor do they "mobilize" the people, create political stability, or help nation-building as the theory suggests.[53] Nevertheless, both the concept of development dictatorship, whose main concern is increased production, and its accompanying attitudes of nationalism, unity, collectivism or communalism, discipline, and state authority, are strongly held in underdeveloped countries.[54]

Certainly the Soviet Union has been rapidly transformed

into a highly modernized country in which the disruption of peasant society has accompanied industrialization.[55] A nation that, in 1917, had only 15 per cent of its population living in towns now contains a population that is 60 per cent urbanized and universally literate. In 1928, 77 per cent of the population were peasants compared with 25 per cent in 1964. The Soviet Union is not only highly industrialized, it has also removed the foreign capital that had dominated Russian industry before the Revolution. That there is an inherent logic in the process of economic modernization—in the sense of increased production, a shift of capital resources and population from agriculture to industry, and greater investment in capital industries—seems undeniable. Yet, if modernization seems a logical step in economic behavior, this does not imply that brutality, dictatorship, or totalitarianism is inevitable or necessary for the attainment of economic objectives. For Stalin, the check on consumption was necessary in order to build up heavy industry, engineering, fuel, and power; and this was to be done only by a policy of forced savings, sacrifice, and ruthless collectivization despite Lenin's argument that collectivization could be satisfactorily achieved only through persuasion.

The economist Alec Nove asked if Stalin was really necessary,[56] but he gave no definitive answer to his own question or to the problem of how much of the arbitrary nature of the Soviet regime was due to the one-party state and centralized planning, and how much to Stalin's peculiarities of character and his errors, such as the attempt to transform "nature," to dig unnecessary canals, build useless railroads in the Arctic, or utilize forced labor camps.[57] The fact that developing nations may be attracted by some characteristics of the Soviet regime—the speed of industrialization, state planning of investment and accumulation of capital, a single party or political movement that can ensure loyalty to the regime, the elimination of illiteracy—does not, however, imply that they must follow the same pattern of political development.

Indeed, the case for the pattern is fallacious. The supposed economic justification for Stalin's collectivization policy was false,[58] since the figures he used were false, and agricultural production had not decreased to the degree he had said. The compulsion was not only irrational, it was irrelevant. Incorrect price and fiscal policies combined with incorrect information and agricultural reorganization produced the grain crisis of 1927-28. Coercion was applied while the alternative policy, suggested by Bukharin, of gradual change—by which the example of successful projects would induce peasants to join collective units—was ignored.

The Party in Totalitarian Systems

A third problem in the theory of totalitarianism concerns the central role of the party. As a logical corollary, the weakness of the party, among other factors, in Portugal and Spain differentiates these nations from the totalitarian regimes. But there was a varying and ambiguous relationship between the party and the state in totalitarian countries. This was first exemplified in Italy with the creation of parallel organs of party and state: Fascist militia alongside the army, special tribunals in addition to the regular courts, federal party secretaries and provincial prefects, the attendance of the party secretary at cabinet meetings, as well as the dual position of Mussolini as Il Duce and head of government. In 1928, it was not some governmental body but the Fascist Grand Council, in reality chosen by Mussolini (who presided over it), which was given the power to nominate individuals from whom his successor would be chosen. The Grand Council not only became a major organ of government but also was able to draw up the electoral lists for the Fascist corporations for which the electorate voted.

The totalitarian party has been regarded as the keeper of the true faith, the agent of the secular religion, and the controller of social relationships and morals. Frequently, the actions of party organs have been outside the legal framework: the regular German courts could not prevent action by the Gestapo or the sending of people to concentration camps without trial. In the Soviet Union, the special tribunals were set up in 1934 to judge "counterrevolutionary crimes," and were not ended until twenty-five years later. Secret police, private armies, paramilitary organizations, special groups in the regular armed forces in the Soviet Union, Nazi Germany, and Fascist Italy exercised power outside of the regular administrative organs.

At the same time, the differentiation between party and state has remained unclear. In the Soviet Union, the communist party is constitutionally "the directing nucleus" of public organizations and government. All government ministers are members of the party and most are also members of its central committee. The Nazi regime was also confusing and chaotic. A Nazi leader might hold a number of party and state positions simultaneously. Among other posts, Goering was Prime Minister of Prussia, Minister of Police for Germany, Commander-in-Chief of the Air Force, head of Television, chairman of the four-year plan, head of forestry.

The true state, for Hitler, was a mighty weapon. But, in 1933, he declared the party to be "the bearer of the Germanic idea of the state and indissolubly mixed with the state." If the Nazi party organizations were not allowed to assume the functions of government, a party decision nevertheless became realistically, if not legally, valid. Party bureaucracy was not always distinguishable from ministerial officials. The party dominated in agricultural and police matters, but not in foreign affairs or over the Wehrmacht. In foreign affairs, the German Foreign Office competed with a number of party groups, such as the Aussenpolitisches Amt under Rosenberg, the Ausland-organisation under Bohle, and the separate group under Ribbentrop.

In addition, the whole concept of political power remained unclear. In 1934, Hitler declared that "it is not the state which gives orders to us, but we who give orders to the state." Yet, he also said on several occasions that the state "is but one of the forms of organization of the people's life," and that party, state, army, the economic structure, and the administration of justice are of secondary importance since "they are but a means to the preservation of the *Volk*." In reality, the SS at times dominated the state and suppressed any potential opposition to Hitler or itself.[59]

The Nazi regime existed in a nation habituated to strong rule and it was supported by, or at least obtained the acquiescence of, the military establishment, the clerical hierarchy, and the economically powerful groups. This alliance of the traditional social groups with the Nazis allowed the state bureaucracy to be independent of the Nazi party to a considerable degree and to be responsible for the direction of the economy in planning, production, and distribution. Speer, while head of German production, always thought of himself as occupying a nonpolitical job. Often the direct intervention of the party was seen as hostile to the best interests of the state. The party never exerted supreme control over the administration of the state, and party control was generally limited to influence over appointments and to the political education of state officials, though it increased during the war. Until 1943, when guidance officers became responsible for political indoctrination in the forces, the army was an autonomous entity, though it remained under the political control of Hitler. This situation, to which may be added the virtual fiefdoms of the paramilitary organizations, often independent of the party, meant a qualification of the power of the party.

In the Soviet Union, the impact of the party has varied even more. Marx himself provided no analysis of the place or functions of the political party. Such analysis became the subject of bitter contention among the disciples. The Leninist analysis envisaged the capture of political power by a disciplined, revolutionary organization, the smashing of the state power, its replacement by the party implementing the dictatorship of the party over the proletariat, and, ultimately, the dictatorship of an individual over the party.

In 1917, the Bolshevik party was a sect rather than a mass movement. The secretariat consisted of Sverdlov and a few people who could barely keep up with a small correspondence, let alone discipline anyone.[60] It was Lenin's tactical genius and opportunism that enabled the Bolsheviks to seize and retain power, creating a one-party state. Lenin refused to permit any non-Bolshevik group to exist, except, for a short time, the Left Social Revolutionaries. Within two years, all opposition socialist parties had been abolished and censorship imposed. Within the Communist party itself, opposition factions were forbidden: In 1920, the Workers' Opposition, demanding rights for trade unionists, was outlawed. Lenin argued that power could not have been maintained "without the strictest discipline, the truly iron discipline in our party,"[61] and without centralization of authority. His idea of "democratic centralism"—in all party organs, election upward and strict discipline downward as well as acceptance by all of the majority decision once made—allowed the top leaders to control the whole organization and was formally adopted by the party at its sixth congress in 1917.

At first, Lenin thought that members of the party would lead the soviets, not that the party would control the state. He adopted the slogan "All power to the soviets," but quickly dropped it when, out of 822 delegates, only 105 Bolsheviks were elected to the First All-Russian Congress. After a brief period of rule by the soviets, the party organization became the dominant force until Stalin's grip on power was firm. For Stalin political control did not preclude, but presupposed, "conscious and voluntary submission, for only conscious discipline can be truly iron discipline."[62] With individual dictatorship, the party declined in importance, and party meetings became increasingly infrequent. Between 1939 and 1952, no congress was held, the Central Committee of the party rarely met, the secret police was a potent power, and the Stalin secretariat a crucial group.

Under Khrushchev, the power of the party was reasserted in an attempt to control the secret police, state administration, army, industrial managers, and economic planners. Industrial decentralization led to the transfer of economic planners and administrators and their subjection to regional party control. District secretaries of the party were given the task of supervising the collective farms. In 1962, the party machine was reorganized into industrial and agricultural sectors in the hope that output would be increased with more specialized party control. Meetings of the party's Central Committee became occasions for discussion between party leaders and economic and industrial leaders. Increased emphasis was put on the use of party groups to guide mass activities and on the mobilization of voluntary labor to perform local projects and services.[63] With its increase in size, the nature of the party itself changed: The party gained mass support and attempted to recruit a greater proportion of workers, collective farmers, young people, and representatives of national minorities. Only at the end of Khrushchev's rule, with the changes in the organization of the economic councils, did there seem to be an attempt to limit the role of the party.

Since the fall of Khrushchev, a clearer and more meaningful distribution of political functions between the general-secretary of the party and the chairman of the Council of Ministers has been tried. At the twenty-third party congress in 1966, Brezhnev announced the withdrawal of the party cadres from the direct administration of the economy and their return to the role of overseers. At the same time, the 1961 statute, which required that membership of cadres be rotated, was repealed, thus permitting greater professionalization. In the party itself, collective leadership has become more of a reality than ever before, and the Politbureau has become the arena for the resolution of differences rather than the voice of dictatorship. The party also surrendered some control over military matters to the professional officers on whom it is dependent for support; these officers, whose role Khrushchev had strengthened, allowed him to be deposed.[64]

In a similar fashion, the party's control over internal matters has relaxed slightly with the reconstituting and renaming of the People's Control Commissions in 1965, which allow citizens to engage to some extent in the control of economic, administrative, and civic functions. Other voluntary organizations—street committees, sanitary brigades, voluntary militia, comrade courts—perform some social activities under the supervision of the party, though it is improbable that they constitute the outline of the future Communist society or herald the likelihood of the revival of the soviets.

In China, also, the party seems to have played an uneven role and been in continual dispute with other authorities. It was Lin Piao, Minister of Defense, military official, and one of the five vice-chairmen of the party's Central Committee, who formulated the doctrine of the people's state in 1965. It was the political department of the army, not the party, that made the selections for the celebrated little red book, the *Thoughts of Mao*. The series of internal disturbances between 1966 and 1968 have left the party divided and paralyzed, while the military, on their own or in revolutionary committees often controlled by regional and district military commanders, have taken over some provinces of China. In the unstable China of the present time, in which provincial governments have almost ceased to function and the party has lost control over central authorities, army officers have emerged not only as dominant elements or ruling groups in some areas, but also as political conciliators between contending groups and as educational and industrial supervisors. The military comprises over 40 per cent of the membership of the Central Committee chosen in 1969, though it has not, as yet, any representation in the inner Politbureau.

In this setting, the Communist Youth League has been dissolved, party organs have been replaced by the Red Guards, by revolutionary committees of soldiers, revolutionaries, and cadres, or by worker-peasant propaganda teams: "revolutionary rebels" have conflicted with the trade unions, and officials and the "People's Communes" have been attacked. The great leader has encouraged attacks on the party. These have led to the dismissal of most of the Politbureau, the secretariat of the Central Committee, the Central Committee, and local party leaders, and have almost ended the authority of the party, in the hope that the purity of the revolution be restored, the power of bureaucrats and specialists be reduced, and all manifestations of bourgeois behavior—such as material incentives and concern for income—be ended. In China, as in Cuba under Castro, the leader has tried to create the party or state in his own image. Far from regarding the party as the national ruling group, Mao has, from time to time, acted independently of it. The new constitution of the Chinese party, proposed in 1969, reduced the role of the chief organs. The national party congress is to meet only every five years, and the Central Committee has no required definite sessions. This merely legitimized existing practice since the national congress, supposedly an annual event, had not met for eleven years, and the Central Committee had not met for four years.

One of the unstated assumptions of those who have held that the one-party state is the key to rapid modernization and nation-building is the efficiency of such a regime. But the experience of the Nazi and Stalinist regimes does not bear this out. In Germany, even if political command had been total, administrative action had been neither unified nor efficient. A number of studies have shown the rivalries, intrigues, and internal conflicts in the regime. In his book *The Last Days of Hitler*, Hugh Trevor-Roper spoke of "the confusion of private empires, private armies, and private intelligence services," and he saw the Nazi leaders as constituting a royal court rather than a government. The foreign labor program, torn by personal dissensions, was never able to function smoothly.[65] German occupation of Russian territory was incoherent and ineffective.[66] The emphasis on military training in school and the reduction of high school education by one year diminished the effectiveness of the educational system. In the Soviet Union, administrative behavior was subordinated to the unpredictable will of Stalin. Both Djilas and Svetlana Alliluyeva have written of the midnight dinners at which the major decisions were made and which kept administrators from their desks until the following noon.[67] The post-Stalin period has constantly illustrated the fallibility of the party and its leaders; the 1962 Cuban crisis and the 1967 Middle East War are only the most obvious examples.

The Need for a New Concept

Useful though the term has been (despite the above qualifications) for analysis of the Stalin and Hitler periods of power, "totalitarianism" is a less valid tool for the study of contemporary political reality for a number of reasons. The theory ignores or minimizes the peculiar and particular role of Stalin and Hitler in the dictatorships and of extreme terror in the regimes. There is no counterpart in the Communist countries today, not even in China, where it might occasionally be said, "L'état, c'est Mao." To use the concept of totalitarianism for the current Soviet regime does not sufficiently differentiate the system from the earlier period. There is no uncontrollable single leader. There has been a drastic reduction of terror and of the police state, and an increase in the expression of free opinion. Terror is no longer arbitrary as in the Stalinist era. The institutionalization of anxiety, of which Alex Inkeles spoke,[68] is not in evidence, even if the subordination of groups and associations has not entirely ended.

Terror has been reduced in a number of ways; by the abolition of the special board of the Ministry of Internal Affairs that was able to send people to camps without trial, by forbidding security police the right to conduct criminal investigations in their own fashion, by the abolition of secret trials for people accused of crimes against the state, and by depriving military courts of their jurisdiction over civilians. Penalties for violations of labor discipline have been lessened. A number of procedural guarantees have been introduced, the legal system rationalized, and the area of control by the Procurator over judicial and administrative acts has been increased.[69]

The Communist systems remain dictatorships, with the party as the dominant organ. The carrot of a welfare state, material incentives, and increasing consumption have, to some extent, been substituted for the stick of terror. Education, propaganda, censorship, control over the news media, a lack of contact with foreigners, the difficulty of expressing political criticism of officials publicly, the absence of any organized opposition group, a people's militia, social pressure through "popular assembly" courts and other devices—all reinforce the nondemocratic aspects of the regimes. In the Soviet Union, if the trend has been toward greater liberalization and the reduction of coercion, it has not been without fluctuation, as has been shown by the harsh penalties—including the death penalty—extended, in 1961-62, to a number of offenses.

In his re-evaluation of the Soviet Union, Fainsod has called the post-Stalin period one of "rationalized" or "enlightened" totalitarianism because the Communist party retained power, remained the final interpreter of official ideology, and maintained central direction of the economy.[70] But the marked differences of the Khrushchev period from that of his predecessor suggest that the regime was a benevolent despotism rather than an enlightened totalitarianism. Power was exercised collectively, but Khrushchev was the only individual to be a member of all the major political organizations, and he protected himself by installing his personal administrative group in office. His successors, too, have tried to secure their hold on power through the appointment of personal followers; for example, Brezhnev, in 1966, increased the number of those members of the Central Committee of the party who came from his own Ukrainian area and on whose loyalty he could rely.[71]

Economic Changes

The changing economic policies of the Communist countries in the last decade also suggest a changing political regime. Carl Friedrich argues that the economic changes "by no means entail an abandonment of the ultimate monopoly of all decisional power by the top leadership." Certainly, the Communist countries are still controlled economies in which prices are fixed and planning determined centrally to a large degree; yet, the consequences stemming from material and technological development—the greater autonomy of the industrial manager, especially in areas such as electronics, synthetic materials, and certain consumer goods that do not need the degree of centralized control exercised over heavy industry, and the need for a more flexible planning system—are incompatible with the use of the party to maintain control over the planning process.

In the Soviet Union, attention has been paid to reform not only because of the increase in consumer demand but also because of the decrease in the rate of economic growth since 1958, the decline in the productivity of capital, and the agricultural shortages of the last decade (despite Khrushchev's attempts to plow virgin lands, make greater use of chemicals to produce fertilizers, and set up agro-towns). The Communist leaders are faced with the problem of reconciling conflicting demands made on the economy as a result of military needs, foreign aid programs, increased need for capital by industry, and commitment to a high rate of economic growth with the desire of citizens for greater consumption as determined by themselves.

Changes have occurred both in the nature of industrial control and in territorial decentralization. Professor Evsei Liberman has become the symbolic figure for the demand that Communist systems reduce the degree of detailed bureaucratic planning and give industrial managers freedom and incentive. Greater efficiency and improved quality would be attained if profitability were given greater emphasis, with less stress put on quantitative production indices as the measurement of plan fulfillment. The Liberman view, that Soviet factories be managed on a profit basis, has important political implications since the maximization of profits requires the calculation of prices based on opportunity cost in a free or largely free market. In some areas, such as investment in new equipment, alteration of production methods, and making of contracts, managerial freedom has already been largely attained, while the whole economy is marked by a shift from industrial coercion to the use of incentives.

To the Liberman view has been added that of the mathematical economists, a group to which some attention is now paid, who have argued that political decision-making in economic matters should be replaced by objective economic calculation reflecting resources available, consumer demand, and necessary incentives. In the past, obeisance to the Marxist labor theory of value led the Soviet Union to deny or minimize the contribution of capital and land to production, to neglect the cost of capital, to ignore the significance of demand and scarce resources in the determination of price, and to neglect economic marginal analysis. More recent ideological flexibility has resulted in interest charges being imposed on capital and long-term loans with the recognition of capital costs and rent being charged on scarce natural resources. Changes in supply methods have led to wholesale trade in equipment, materials, and semifinished products. Prices in the consumer-goods sector now more truly correspond to costs. Since earnings are currently increasing more rapidly than productivity, bonus payments are being made in relation to productivity. To obtain greater efficiency and to take greater advantage of new technology, larger industrial corporations have been planned.

The nature of the Soviet economy has varied with time and circumstance. From war communism, the result of external and civil war, it changed (with Lenin's insistence) to the New Economic Policy with its use of the market and its encouragement of private initiative to some degree. Then followed the Stalinist policy of forced collectivization, concentration on industry to the detriment of agriculture, centralized planning, and restraints on consumption in order to increase the output of heavy industry, engineering, and military material. In the current economy, access to the market coexists with a central economic plan.

By the logic of its doctrine, a socialist system must be responsible for economic growth and for determining the pace and direction of that growth. Hayek has argued in a number of works[72] that a regime aiming at the implementing of particular social ends must end in totalitarianism; yet, there does not appear to be any automatic reason for this either generally in theory or specifically in the Soviet Union. Centralized planning began after the Revolution without any theoretical formulation but influenced by the example of Imperial Germany,[73] the first planned economy in modern times, and conditioned by the needs of war communism, with its concentrated purpose of survival.

The Communist countries are undergoing a transitional process, from direct central control over the economy to more indirect means of control, while maintaining their planning objectives. After the fiftieth anniversary of the Revolution, the Soviet Union is evaluating the desirability of profits and profit-sharing, both in itself and as a criterion for policy-making, interest rates and capital charges, rent, advertising, installment credit, and overseas investment, as well as a new emphasis on material incentives.[74] Hayek's argument is disproved by the alternation in the Communist systems between collective control and material incentives, party control over the economy and increased individual decision-making and managerial independence.

The need to respond to practical requirements despite any ideological misgivings has been shown in agricultural matters both in the Soviet Union and in China. Restrictions on private property by Stalin and Khrushchev affected the socialist sector adversely. Agricultural crises have, since 1964, obliged the Soviet Union to take measures to expand private production by increasing the average size of plot of the kolkhoz member and the size of private plots formed by members of collective farms.[75] In China, too, despite Maoist indoctrination and socialist education campaigns, peasants still demand private plots and free markets and advocate the breaking up of communes into more viable units.

Considerable discussion has taken place recently on the question of the convergence of the highly developed capitalist and Communist countries due to the functional imperatives of industrialism.[76] Both sets of systems have complex, sophisticated economies, which require economic planning as well as flexibility, a considerable degree of governmental regulation, and some element of public control. The degree of central planning in Yugoslavia and Czechoslovakia has not been much greater than in a capitalist country such as France. Nevertheless, important differences remain between the systems—differences regarding the form of ownership, the method of regulating the economy and allocating resources, and the distribution of wealth.[77]

One of the great dangers in a highly centralized economy is that the decision load on a government may be greater than the means and ability of that government to deal with it, as Karl Deutsch has warned.[78] The Communist countries have sought to avoid this dilemma by using differing forms of decentralization. In the Soviet Union, over 100 regional economic councils were established by Khrushchev in 1957 when the industrial ministries were abolished. The regional structure was largely ended by his successors with the restoration of the ministries in 1965, but preparatory proposals for the next five-year plan (1970-75) envisage a larger role for regional authorities since the central planners will lay down only broad lines of development. Already, many exceptions to the general rules laid down in the state plan have been found to be necessary in practice: An increasing proportion of capital investment is in the hands of managers; retailers have much greater freedom in ordering stock.

Decentralization has gone further in other Communist systems. Since 1953, nationalized enterprises in Yugoslavia have competed against each other in a kind of "market socialism" in which the government sets the goals and targets and retains control over prices and materials, but individual enterprises are able to decide their own production plans, prices, and how profits are to be allocated. Wages and profits depend on productivity. There is a certain degree of freedom in the capital market. Banking is not interfered with politically, and even a stock exchange has recently been discussed. Ownership and control have been decentralized: In 1965, the government agreed that most of the decision on capital spending at the federal, republic, or commune level should be made the responsibility of the enterprises themselves. Workers have participated in management to an increasing degree, with the managerial director acting under the control of a workers' council, though liberals still complain about bureaucratic interference by party and government officials.

Other Communist countries have, to some degree, experimented with the profit motive as the method by which to obtain greater efficiency and have also taken greater account of consumer demands. Czechoslovakia has a central policy-making economic body but also considerable decentralization of industry and management and autonomy of individual state enterprises that compete for markets and credits. At the same time, factory managers still do not determine the basic wages of their workers even if they do influence them through bonuses and by providing housing and other benefits. In Hungary, price reform is in a transitional period, while greater freedom has been allowed in import and export trade. Rumania has recently allowed greater autonomy to individual enterprises, which are being grouped together into trusts directly responsible to a minister, and which can plan their own production programs and techniques.

All this is not to deny that the Communist countries still manifest the presence of strong controls, the maintenance of administrative allocation of materials, the limitation of incentives, the linking of managerial bonuses to profits by administrative decree. They are still characterized by real or simulated commitment to the principles of Marxism-Leninism, though the interpretation of the sacred texts is open to continual discussion, and by the controlled interdependence of economic, social, cultural, administrative, and political institutions. Politically, they are closed societies, to use the dichotomy of open-closed systems that Popper and others have suggested. Economically, they are command economies with many detailed targets set by the administration.[79] Even the Soviet Central Planning Agency acts by reference to political leaders rather than according to technical criteria. The Russian manager has not yet become an independent decision-maker.

Political Changes

Even admitting that political controls over the economy are still strong in the Communist countries, the economic and political changes that are under way suggest that a classification other than totalitarianism is desirable. The regimes have sought devices by which power can be controlled. In Yugoslavia, no individual is permitted to hold senior positions in both party and government, and the security police has been reduced. While in power, Khrushchev proposed the compulsory retirement of a certain percentage of officials: one-third of the deputies to the Supreme Soviet were to be replaced and one-quarter of the members of the Soviet Presidium and the Central Committee were to retire after each election, though the decisions on the persons to be chosen for retirement were to be made by the party secretary. Not surprisingly, the proposal was withdrawn after Khrushchev's downfall.

Communist parliaments have played a larger role in recent years, though small by comparison with that played in democratic systems. Parliamentary committees have been more active, including the specialized committees in the Soviet Union. Other features of free societies have been haltingly developing. Czechoslovakia, in 1968, was contemplating a new electoral law providing for alternative candidates, though within the National Front, for every post; all elections were to be by secret ballot. In the chambers comprising the Yugoslav assemblies, specialists have been exerting greater influence. Courts, especially in Yugoslavia, have acted as restraints on administrative actions. Most remarkable of all was the offer to resign made by the Prime Minister of Slovenia, in 1966, after the government had been defeated on a legislative bill—even though the offer was later withdrawn.

These changes allow one to raise the question—unthinkable a few years ago—of the possibility of tolerated public opposition in the Communist world, with the end of belief in the infallibility of leadership. In the Communist movements of the West, this possibility has been accepted. The Italian Communist party, recommending the possibility of a parliamentary road to communism, has argued both that factions may legitimately coexist within the party and that non-Communist parties may continue to exist after the Communist capture of power. During the 1960's, the student group within the French Communist organization opposed the official leadership of the party. Within the Soviet Union, the articulation of public criticism of governmental action, limited though it is, suggests a regime different from the one characterized by "the passion for unanimity" of which Friedrich and Brzezinski once spoke.

Liberalization in the Soviet Union has been an uneven process, and the thaw has cooled from time to time. In 1966, this was shown by the severe Soviet decrees on law and order and the handling of crime. Kremlinologists might take the promotion of Semichastny, director of the police since 1962, to full membership of the Central Committee, and of Shelepin, director before 1962, to full membership in the Politbureau, and the appointment of General Shchelokov to head the Ministry for the Preservation of Public Order as symbolic of an increase in the power of police officials. The invasion of Czechoslovakia in 1968, though defended as necessary to meet "counter-revolution," indicated that too great a degree of free expression would not be tolerated. Even in Yugoslavia, the limits of freedom have been shown both by the treatment of Djilas for his critical analysis of the regime and of Mihajlov, the writer who, in 1966, was imprisoned for planning a conference to launch a new periodical of a democratic-social nature that was to constitute a loyal opposition in the regime.

The argument of Friedrich suggests, by implication, both that the current thaw is part of the continual oscillations and zigzags the Soviet Union has experienced and that oppression may well recur in the future. It may be so, but a number of factors can be taken into account. The first is the genuine revulsion felt by the Soviet political elite and the intelligentsia at the crimes of the Stalinist period and against barbaric behavior in a modern society. Another is that a highly industrialized, scientifically sophisticated and militarily nonbelligerent regime requires political stability and moderation. In international affairs, the existence of nuclear weapons and the Sino-Soviet dispute have led the Soviet Union to a policy of peaceful coexistence with the West. In addition, the impact of international public opinion in general and of the United Nations in particular has led the Soviet Union

to have a more decent respect for the opinions of
mankind.

Intellectual Dissent

The intellectual monopoly, reinforced by concentration
camps for opponents, which was characteristic of the past,
has become less rigid. But dissent has not been allowed to
go too far and internal emigration is still prevalent. Russian
students still complain that art is made tongue-tied by
authority. The continuation of Soviet censorship of
literature, art, and music, the ungenerous treatment of
Pasternak, the fulminations of the politician Semichastny
and the writer Sholokhov and the bureaucrats of the
Writers' Union, against the critics of the regime, the
imprisonment of Sinyavsky, Daniel, Tarsis, and Brodsky,
the arrest of those writers who publicly criticized the trial
of the first two and the arrest of Budovsky, who in turn
had criticized the condemnation of these critics, all sadly
show this. Similar actions were taken in other countries, as
in Poland, when the production of Adam Mickiewicz's
nineteenth-century play *The Forefathers* was ended
because of the applause greeting the anti-Russian passages
in it.

Yet *Novy Mir* and its courageous editor Tvardovsky,
Solzhenitsyn, who had asked for the complete abolition of
censorship, Pavel Litvinov and other scientists in the Soviet
Union, and, in Poland, Kolakowski, Kuron, and Modzelew-
ski have dared to articulate a more critical or unorthodox
view of the system, to display some independence of the
ruling political authorities, and to call for independent
organizations as well as for intellectual freedom, even if
they have been punished for these critical views. A petition
signed by sixty-three writers in 1966 asked that Sinyavsky
and Daniel not be sentenced to prison; in 1968, great
protest greeted the trial of Galanskov and Ginzburg. More

attention is being paid to the early humanistic works of Marx and, therefore, to the problems of the individual. Writers, artists, and scientists have all been concerned with genuine intellectual inquiry, and they often have little in common with the party bureaucrats who are less well educated and who tend to come from a lower-class or peasant background. It is a sign of the changing times that these writers have not been subjected to severe physical violence or to death, as in the cases of Mandelshtam, Babel, Pilnyak, and Vasilyev. The Communist regimes no longer conform to the totalitarian pattern in which, as Kolakowski said, "philosophers and writers always say the same thing as generals and ministers, but always after them."

The Changing Communist World

The concept of totalitarianism, if applied automatically to all the Communist countries, disregards not only the changing nature of the Soviet Union but also the diversity of the different regimes in which changes have occurred at varying rates. The Soviet Union has been trying to alter its own self-image. At the twenty-second party congress in 1961, the Soviet state was proclaimed to be the state of the whole people, and thus, transformed from one based on the dictatorship of the proletariat. In the realm of international affairs, the insistence on the need for peaceful coexistence with the capitalist countries and on the fact that war is not fatalistically inevitable suggests the surrender of any theory of permanent revolution externally as well as internally.

The concept also tends to ignore the differences, based partly on conflicting interpretations of Marxism but largely on clashing national interests, between the Communist countries. The countries vary—from a Poland in which politics cannot ignore religious beliefs and ecclesiastical

authorities to a Yugoslavia, which has not attempted to
introduce collectivization measures. Yugoslavia under Tito
is less a totalitarian than a dictatorial regime. Even the
party is national only at the level of the Central Committee of the federation; at all other levels, it is composed of
units from each of the six republics making up the
country. Yugoslavia has pioneered reforms in a number of
ways: by the workers' self-management program, by the
autonomy of labor organizations, by a federal structure in
which the republics have some real powers, by the
separation of the political function from the administrative, by the periodic renewal of members of representative
assemblies and important officeholders, and by constitutional guarantees and protective devices, including the
Federal Constitutional Court set up in 1964. Some years
ago, Waldermar Gurian spoke of totalitarian movements as
secularized religions or ideocracies.[80] Attractive though
Marxist ideology may still be to some, it can no longer be
regarded as a substitute religion, except for those Chinese
seeking to produce a cultural revolution. The Communist
world has witnessed ideological fragmentation, including
the opportunism of Khrushchev, the patriotism of Tito,
the revisionism of Togliatti, the nationalism of the Poles.
More numerous than those calling for international revolution are the advocates of a parliamentary road to a new
society, of internal majority and minority factions, and
even of opposition parties. In a state of such fragmentation
and change, it is not very useful to insist on the concept of
totalitarianism.

Group Conflicts

The concept also tended to neglect factional conflicts
within the ruling party. The concept is based on the
premise that the one-party system is monolithic, coherent,
and united in doctrinal persuasion and in political action.

But the very division of opinion within the ruling party and the presence of group pressures suggest that the party, as Aron wrote some years ago, should be regarded as "monopolistic" rather than monolithic.[81]

Under totalitarian regimes, considerable autonomy has always been present in an area like science, partly because of its intrinsic utility and partly because it is not likely to threaten the basic principles of the regime. Science, in turn, has been accorded great prestige and dignity, financial benefits, and government support. The Soviet educational system, which is allocated about 7 per cent of the gross national product, is, to a great degree, concerned with producing scientific and engineering students, but substantial freedom has been allowed a number of disciplines—such as physics and biology—which have the most rigorous academic requirements, or which seem to be remote from practical application, such as sensory physiology.[82]

Friedrich and Brzezinski spoke of "islands of separateness" such as the family, the universities, and the military, those areas of social and cultural activity from which a certain amount of opposition emanates in the totalitarian system. Nevertheless, the general impression remained of a monolithic structure in which dissent rarely disturbed existing unanimity. In fact, the Byzantine party squabbles of which we have become aware in the post-Stalin Soviet Union do not seem of a different nature from those in Mississippi, Manhattan, or Cook County. Many recent writings on the Soviet Union have emphasized the presence and significance of interest groups. The Communist party itself has become the place for resolution of conflicting interests. Decision-makers in the Soviet Union take account of the views of groups such as managers, consumers, intellectuals, different sections of the bureaucracy, the military, scientists, trade unions, farmers, youth, and the various non-Russian nationalities. Not only do groups such as these participate in the running of a modern society but they also constitute "plural checks" on the exercise of power and form the basis for criticizing existing policy.[83]

In the confusing picture of modern China, the political kaleidoscope has included divisions within the party and the army, local factions, the activity of—and the resistance to—teams composed of workers, soldiers, and peasants, the existence of a political court and intriguers, wives of leaders wielding influence as royal mistresses did in the past. No monolithic entity exists in a party where Liu Shao-chi, the careful organizer, could for years be at odds with Mao Tse-tung, the revolutionary romantic and proponent of continual struggle.

NAZISM AND COMMUNISM

Underlying the concept of totalitarianism has been the tendency to equate nazism and communism or at least to imply that the similarities between the two regimes that purported to incorporate these philosophies were greater than their differences. The many similarities are undeniable, and Friedrich was right to emphasize the role of violence in both systems. Aggressiveness, militarism, emphasis on national strength, anti-Semitism were to be found in all the totalitarian systems. As late as 1962, the publication in the Soviet Union of certain essays by Baron Holbach suggested a policy of deliberate anti-Semitism. Fascist desire for territorial aggrandizement can be compared with the idea of "the third Rome," the civilizing mission of the Russians. Peter Viereck once called "National Bolshevism the cousin to German National Socialism," and Raymond Aron suggested a comparison between the Communist myth of the Revolution and the Fascist cult of violence. Hitler's view that art should be intelligible to the masses coincided with the Soviet view of "socialist realism."

Nevertheless, the totalitarian concept does not sufficiently allow for the enormously different purposes sought by the three ideologies or beliefs, for the different intellectual levels of those beliefs, for the different styles of behavior and symbolic references of the regimes, and for the different groups who supported and benefited by them. Totalitarianism of the left, as Talmon has argued, begins with man, his rationality, and salvation; totalitarianism of the right begins with the collective entity—the state, the nation, or the race.

To offer brief lists of the major characteristics of the belief systems is to illustrate their different purposes. Nazism was characterized by nationalism, racism, emphasis on the *Volk*, anti-Semitism, stress on violence and force, appeal to national unity that would supersede the interests and differences of rank and class. With its rejection of democracy, secularization, rationalism, and positivism, its belief in domestic virtues, its vision of an attractive mythical past and rural harmony, its distaste for industrial civilization and urbanism, nazism was the counterrevolution in action and ultimately nihilistic in nature. The precapitalist, feudal aspects of nazism are illustrated by its Teutonic imagery, elitist decision-making through the Führer and the Gauleiter appointed by him, the oath of personal loyalty to Hitler, the stress on honor, blood, and soil, the end to the dependence of the German peasant on the market economy.[84] Ernst Nolte has commented that, while Italian fascism recalled a remote but tangible historical era, the Nazis appealed to the prehistoric and the archaic.[85]

The Nazis drew their main strength from the lower-middle class, marginal groups, military desperados, and those who had suffered by greater industrialization. But, uninterested in changing the nature of the social order, the Nazis were prepared to cooperate with those traditional groups such as the military and the bureaucracy that were not regarded as opponents. Though some 40 per cent of the full professors in economics and the social sciences vacated their chairs between 1932 and 1938, many academics, jurists, and even Nobel Prize winners capitulated before the regime. Hitler, in March, 1933, spoke of his regime as "the union between the symbols of the old greatness and the new strength." And the new strength was based on the manipulation of crowds, the display of strength through demonstrations, parades, and mass meetings, the welding of what Hitler, in *Mein Kampf*, called "the enormous human dragon" into a potent political force.

Contrasted with these characteristics are the ends of Marxism: that it seeks a society based on equality and humanitarianism, that it envisages the elimination of political coercion, that it seeks to build a rational social order, an industrialized economy, a higher form of democracy than that existing in the capitalist countries, and that it seeks to create a new type of civilization, internationalist rather than insular and parochial in nature. The traditional social and economic elite groups have no place in such a civilization or new type of society, and a wholly new political instrument is necessary. That the Communist regime distorted these high expectations and ended political liberty is not to deny the loftiness of the ideas.

The differentiation between a counterrevolutionary and a revolutionary purpose is crucial in the evaluation of the Nazi and Communist regimes. The objective of the first remains negative—the downfall of the existing regime—or nebulous, depending on the will of the dictator. The regime is essentially a destructive one in which positive achievement is gratuitous or related only to some destructive function. It is the product of a real dilemma of liberal democracy, a sort of suicidal reaction against a civilization that had failed to provide sufficient emotional satisfaction or material benefits for the mass of the people. In no real way can nazism or fascism be regarded as the continuation or inheritance of the French Revolution. The Nazi movement, as Rauschning wrote,[86] had no fixed aims, either economic or political, either in domestic or foreign affairs. Its strength lay in incessant activity, its Valhalla the lust for power and the quest for adventure.

For Communist countries, the creation of an equalitarian and humane society, while not necessarily observed in practice, is its informing spirit, and action can be related to that fundamental objective. The Russian Revolution began, Deutscher noted, "with the dazzling blaze of a great vision."[87] There is no inherent insistence on violence in the Communist, as in the Nazi or Fascist, system. In the post-Stalin Communist systems, violence is an incidental factor, a means by which to achieve a desired end. But violence was an intrinsic facet of Nazi or Fascist behavior, unrelated to rational purpose. In Italy, the aggressive defenders of "law and order in the streets" and the strikebreakers became the *squadrista*. For Hitler, "force was the first law" and war, the normal condition of mankind. The means as well as the ends of the regimes were different in theory. The Nazi and Fascist regimes saw themselves as perpetual dictatorships from the beginning. The Bolsheviks took power on behalf of the Soviet of Workers' and Soldiers' Deputies, and the dictatorship of the proletariat has always been regarded as a transitional stage toward a free society.

In his essay in this volume, Friedrich seems to imply that George Sorel's call for violence is relevant to the Marxist doctrine of the class struggle. But Sorel, although at one point an advocate of revolutionary syndicalism and, at the end of his life in 1922, an admirer of Lenin, was a complex political thinker who can be claimed by the right as well as by the left. His arguments for creative violence, displays of heroism, use of myth, spontaneity of proletarian movements, and syndicalist society where the worker was producer, not surprisingly led him to regard the Fascists as an elite and Mussolini as a political genius. Mussolini himself, in his 1932 Encyclopedia article, indicated the importance of Sorel in the origins of fascism.

At the same time, the ambiguity of the Sorelian position is indicative of the fact that there is no simple dichotomy between left and right in the contemporary world. Friedrich shrewdly points out that many of the Nazi themes have reappeared in the influential work of Franz Fanon. It is not coincidental that Fanon's work has been attractive both to neo-Marxists such as Jean-Paul Sartre and Che Guevera, as far as its stress on revolutionary guerrilla war is concerned, and also to black nationalists, in Africa as well as in the United States, who have appropriated its passages on racism, violence, and lack of compromise and converted them into what appears to be a new form of destructive black fascism.

AN END TO TOTALITARIANISM

For all these reasons, the concept of totalitarianism is no longer the most useful classificatory device for the study of current Communist systems. One must acknowledge that the term has been valuable in the past and that it still possesses utility for analysis of the Chinese regime and those regimes adhering to the Chinese position in the Sino-Soviet dispute. Yet, Friedrich's desire to keep the concept, with amended definition, to apply to the Soviet and Eastern European systems, and his brilliant attempt to justify this, has led him to a shaky methodological position. He argues that "totalitarianism" is a relative category, and that a regime can be more or less totalitarian. But one must ask "relative to what?" The concept was formulated to differentiate the unique behavior of two, or possibly three, states from other autocratic or authoritarian systems. When two of these three regimes have collapsed and the third has witnessed some crucial changes, the term seems hardly applicable. Totalitarianism, after all, has no ontological or essentialist element about it.

There remains the problem of how best to analyze the Communist regimes—either as individual systems or as a group or within the general rubric of comparative politics. This problem has aroused considerable discussion in recent years, and a number of alternative methods have been suggested. As a unique bloc, the Communist systems can be analyzed within the context of area studies or through the examination of certain themes or factors pertinent to them all, such as the manner in which power is exercised by and within the party, the nature of ideology, industrial and agricultural organization, the role of groups such as the bureaucracy, police, or intelligentsia.[88] Within the framework of comparative politics, the most interesting suggestions have been to study the Soviet system as an example of economic modernization and political development, as a mature industrial society with problems similar to those in other developed societies, as a bureaucratic dictatorship, and as a prominent example of a one-party system.

As the prototype of a society moving rapidly to a high level of industrialization, the history of the Soviet Union illustrates, and can be compared with, the efforts made by the underdeveloped countries to build a nation and to integrate various groups within it, to plan for economic growth, and to mobilize resources. Some have wondered if Marxist theory is not more appropriate for a developing, than for a highly industrialized, system.

The present industrial and military capacity of the Soviet Union and the maturity of its society allows comparison with Western developed nations on subjects common to both.[89] These might include political and administrative organization, urbanization, education, allocation of resources, automation, crime, the meaningfulness of basic beliefs, and social stratification as the regime becomes more concerned with managerial activities than with building the system, with reconciling group interests, and with attending to consumer demands. Soviet development led to the formulation of the "convergence theory": that the Soviet Union and the United States were steadily converging toward a similar type of social organization and economy. Suggested by Sorokin in 1944, this thesis has been extensively discussed by Aron, Duverger, Rostow, Tinbergen, and Brzezinski and Huntington, among others.

The complaint that citizens have no control over their destiny or are not consulted by their rulers is familiar in the West, and has now led to demands in many countries for participation in government. Alfred Meyer[90] has been one of the main proponents of the analysis of the Soviet Union as a bureaucratic system, an authoritarian political structure in which the elite escape control by the conformist masses. The expectation of a classless society is regarded as illusory. In this view, the Soviet Union may be best understood—after the initial period of a more terrorist totalitarianism that was used in the crash program of industrialization—as a large, complex bureaucracy comparable in structure and function to large organizations in general. Organizational behavior has become routinized and predictable as ideology has become taken for granted. The system is more dependent on material rewards, such as benefits, social services, or a regressive tax, and sanctions than on the minimal rewards and the expendability of human beings characteristic of the past. The fact that the bureaucracy is highly politicized does not deny the utility of the bureaucratic model for analysis.

The argument of Trotsky and, more recently, of Djilas

that a new class of bureaucrats had been created in the Soviet Union, constituting the real ruling group, overemphasizes the homogeneity or unity of such a group. But, clearly, it is even more valid here than for the Western countries to argue that a small political elite possesses advantages denied to the masses. Hannah Arendt tried to portray the banality of evil of the Nazi regime through an Eichmann who, in spite of his ability to define Kant's categorical imperative correctly, could say that "administrative language is the only language I know." The loyal, unquestioning bureaucrat is the base on which both the Nazi and the Soviet regime have rested.

In a similar argument, Allen Kassof[91] has suggested that the Soviet Union be seen as an administered society, a totalism without terror, whose organization, coordination, and desire to remove conflicts are based on supposed social and historical laws, and in which a political directorate controls planning and direction in the name of welfare and progress. The Soviet bureaucracy, in its desire to preserve the status quo, is a conservative force, an example of institutional and behavioral ossification; not surprisingly, it is an example Mao has not been prepared to accept as representing the future of China.

Robert Tucker[92] has argued very cogently that the Soviet Union could be analyzed as falling within the category of "a revolutionary mass-movement regime under single party auspices." This would allow the Communist regime to be compared with Fascist and with nationalist single party regimes, since all possess a philosophy of revolution, a program of revolutionary struggle, a militant revolutionary party, and a program of national renewal. In the new edition of her influential book, *The Origins of Totalitarianism*, Hannah Arendt also has suggested that the Soviet Union might now be regarded as a one-party dictatorship rather than as a totalitarian system. The differences between the one-party regimes of the Communist systems and those of the developing nations of Africa and Asia are immense; yet, the relevance of such an analysis is shown by the fact that, as John Kautsky has argued,[93] communism in underdeveloped countries is not easily distinguishable from the nationalist and modernizing movements led by intellectuals in those countries.

Each of these approaches illustrates a facet of the past or current behavior of the Soviet Union and invites comparison with other political systems; none illuminates the system as a whole. The desire to relate the Soviet system to modern political analysis is wholly salutary, but does not entail the acceptance of any one particular model. Above all, it does not serve the cause of comparative political analysis or of political understanding to cling to the concept of totalitarianism.

NOTES

1. Herbert J. Spiro and Benjamin R. Barber, "The Concept of 'Totalitarianism' as the Foundation of American Counter-Ideology in the Cold War," a paper presented at the 1967 Annual Meeting of the American Political Science Association.

2. George F. Kennan, *Memoirs, 1925-50* (Boston: Little, Brown, 1967), pp. 358-63.

3. Arthur Koestler, *The Yogi and the Commissar* (New York: Macmillan, 1967), p. 177.

4. George F. Kennan, "The Russian Revolution—Fifty Years After: Its Nature and Consequence," *Foreign Affairs*, XLVI (October, 1967), p. 20.

5. Max Beloff, *The Age of Absolutism: 1660-1815* (New York: Harper & Row, 1966).

6. Giovanni Gentile, "The Philosophic Basis of Fascism," *Foreign Affairs*, VI (January, 1928), p. 299.

7. Richard Lowenthal, "Totalitarianism Reconsidered," *Commentary*, XXIX (June, 1960), pp. 506-7.

8. Hannah Arendt, *Between Past and Future* (Cleveland, Ohio: World Publishing, 1963); also, "Authority in the 20th Century," *Review of Politics*, XVIII (October, 1956), pp. 403-17.

9. William Kornhauser, *The Politics of Mass Society* (Chicago: The Free Press of Glencoe, 1959); Harold Lasswell, "The Psychology of Hitlerism," in his *The Analysis of Political Behavior* (Hamden, Conn: Shoe String Press, 1947); Hadley Cantril, *The Politics of Despair* (New York: Basic Books, 1958); J. L. Talmon, *The Origins of Totalitarian Democracy* (New York: Frederick A. Praeger, 1961).

10. Stanley G. Payne, *Falange: A History of Spanish Fascism* (Stanford, Calif.: Stanford University Press, 1967), p. 224.

11. Maximiano Venero, *La Falange en la guerra de España* (Paris: Ruedo Ibérico, 1968).

12. George Hills, *Franco* (New York: Macmillan, 1967), p. 380.

13. H. R. Trevor-Roper, "The Phenomenon of Fascism," in S. J. Woolf (ed.), *European Fascism* (London: Weidenfeld & Nicolson, 1968), pp. 18-38.

14. For the controversy over Plato see Renford Bambrough (ed.), *Plato, Popper and Politics* (New York: Barnes & Noble, 1967).

15. Carl Friedrich and Zbigniew Brzezinski, *Totalitarian Dictatorship and Autocracy*, Rev. ed. (New York: Frederick A. Praeger, 1967).

16. Gaetano Salvemini, *Under the Axe of Fascism* (New York: Viking, 1936).

17. Quoted in Eugen Weber, "Nationalism, Socialism and National-Socialism in France," *French Historical Studies*, II (Spring, 1962).

18. Hajo Holborn, "Origins and Political Character of Nazi Ideology," *Political Science Quarterly*, LXXIX (December, 1964), pp. 542-54.

19. Herbert Luethy, "The Wretched Little Demon that was Hitler," *Commentary*, XVII (February, 1954), pp. 129-38.

20. Fritz Tobias, *The Reichstag Fire* (London: Secker & Warburg, 1963).

21. Hermann Rauschning, *Germany's Revolution of Destruction* (London: Heinemann, 1939), pp. 58-62.

22. Abram Tertz (Andrey Sinyavsky), *On Socialist Realism* (New York: Pantheon, 1960).

23. Karl Mannheim, *Ideology and Utopia* (New York: Harcourt, 1936).

24. H. R. Trevor-Roper, *Men and Events* (New York: Harper & Bros., 1957), p. 296.

25. Marshall Goldman, "Trade and the Consumer," *Survey*, LXIV (July, 1967), pp. 129-42.

26. Alec Nove, "Ideology and Agriculture," *Soviet Studies*, XVII (April, 1966), pp. 397-407.

27. George F. Kennan, *Russia, The Atom and the West* (New York: Harper & Bros., 1958), p. 22.

28. Stalin, *Marxism and Problems of Linguistics* (Moscow: State Publishing House, 1951-52).

29. Joseph Berliner, "Marxism and the Soviet Economy," *Problems of Communism*, XIII (September, 1964), pp. 1-11.

30. H. F. Schurmann, "Peking's Recognition of Crisis," *Problems of Communism*, X (September-October, 1961), pp. 5-14.

31. Robert J. Lifton, *Thought Reform and the Psychology of Totalism* (New York: W. W. Norton, 1961); also Chalmers Johnson, "China; the Cultural Revolution in Structural Perspective," *Asian Survey*, VIII (January, 1968), pp. 1-15.

32. Denis Mack Smith, *Italy, a Modern History* (Ann Arbor: University of Michigan Press, 1959), p. 44.

33. Franz Von Papen, *Memoirs* (New York: E. P. Dutton, 1953), p. 259.

34. Robert E. MacMaster, *Danilevsky, a Russian Totalitarian Philosopher* (Cambridge, Mass.: Harvard University Press, 1967).

35. Franco Venturi, *Roots of Revolution* (New York: Alfred A. Knopf, 1960), pp. 389-428.

36. Crane Brinton, *The Anatomy of Revolution* (New York: Random House, Vintage ed., 1965).

37. Talmon, *op. cit.*

38. J. L. Talmon, *The Unique and the Universal* (New York: George Braziller, 1965), p. 210.

39. Robert Conquest, *The Great Terror* (New York: Macmillan, 1968), p. xiv.

40. Hannah Arendt, *The Origins of Totalitarianism*, Rev. ed. (Cleveland, Ohio: World Publishing, Meridian ed., 1958), introduction.

41. Quoted in J. J. Marie, *Staline 1879-1953* (Paris: Editions du Seuil, 1967).

42. Mao Tse-tung, *An Anthology of His Writings*, ed. Anne Fremantle (New York: Mentor, 1962), p. 274.

43. Boris Nikolaevsky, *Power and the Soviet Elite* (New York: Frederick A. Praeger, 1965), p. 44.

44. Sidney Hook, "Whither Russia?" *Problems of Communism*, XVI (March-April, 1967), p.78.

45. Merle Fainsod, *How Russia is Ruled*, Rev. ed. (Cambridge, Mass.: Harvard University Press, 1963), p. 421.

46. Z. K. Brzezinski, "The Nature of the Soviet System," *Slavic Review*, XX (October, 1961), pp. 351-68.

47. Robert T. Holt and John E. Turner, *The Political Basis of Economic Development* (Princeton, N.J.: Van Nostrand, 1966), p. 15.

48. Czeslaw Milosz, *The Captive Mind* (New York: Alfred A. Knopf, 1953), p. 215.

49. Hannah Arendt, *Eichmann in Jerusalem* (New York: Viking, 1963), and comments in Carl J. Friedrich (ed.), *Totalitarianism* (Cambridge, Mass.: Harvard University Press, 1954), p. 337.

50. Isaac Deutscher, *Russia in Transition*, Rev. ed. (New York: Grove Press, 1960); A. F. Organski, *The Stages of Political Development* (New York: Alfred A. Knopf, 1965); W. W. Rostow, *The Stages of Economic Growth* (New York: Cambridge University Press, 1960).

51. Lewis Coser, "Prospects for the New Nations: Totalitarianism, Authoritarianism or Democracy," in Coser (ed.), *Political Sociology* (New York: Harper & Row, 1967), p. 271.

52. Raymond Aron (ed.), *World Technology and Human Destiny* (Ann Arbor: University of Michigan Press, 1963), p. 14.

53. Samuel Finer, "The One-Party Regimes in Africa: Reconsiderations," *Government and Opposition*, II (July, 1967), pp. 491-509.

54. A. James Gregor, "African Socialism, Socialism and Fascism: An Appraisal," *Review of Politics*, XXIX (July, 1967), pp. 324-53.

55. David Mitrany, *Marx against the Peasant* (Chapel Hill, N.C.: University of North Carolina, 1952).

56. Alec Nove, *Was Stalin Really Necessary?* (London: Allen & Unwin, 1964), pp. 17-39.

57. Alec Nove, "Thoughts on Irrationality and Waste," *Survey*, LXIV (July, 1967), pp. 143-58.

58. Jerzy F. Karcz, "Thoughts on the Grain Problem," *Soviet Studies*, XVIII (April, 1967), pp. 399-434.

59. H. Krausnick, H. Buchheim, M. Broszat, and H. A. Johnson, *Anatomy of the SS State* (New York: Walker, 1968).

60. Robert V. Daniels, "The Bolshevik Gamble," *The Russian Review*, XXVI (October, 1967), pp. 331-40.

61. Lenin, *"Left-Wing" Communism: An Infantile Disorder* (London: Lawrence & Wishart, 1942), pp. 8-9.

62. Stalin, *Foundations of Leninism* (London: Lawrence & Wishart, 1942), pp. 113-14.

63. Howard Swearer, "Popular Participation: Myths and Realities," *Problems of Communism*, IX (September-October, 1960), pp. 42-51.

64. Roman Kolkowicz, *The Soviet Military and the Communist Party* (Princeton, N.J.: Princeton University Press, 1967).

65. Edward Homze, *Foreign Labor in Nazi Germany* (Princeton, N.J.: Princeton University Press, 1967), p. 311.

66. Gerald Reitlinger, *The House Built on Sand* (New York: Viking, 1960).

67. Milovan Djilas, *Conversations with Stalin* (New York: Harcourt, Brace & World, 1963); Svetlana Alliluyeva, *Twenty Letters to a Friend* (New York: Harper & Row, 1967).

68. Alex Inkeles, "The Totalitarian Mystique: Some Impressions of the Dynamics of Totalitarian Society," in Carl Friedrich (ed.), *Totalitarianism, op. cit.*, pp. 87-108.

69. Harold Berman, "The Dilemma of Soviet Law Reform," *Harvard Law Review*, LXXVI (March, 1963), pp. 929-51.

70. Merle Fainsod, " 'Rationalized' Totalitarianism," in Howard R. Swearer and Richard Longaker (eds.), *Contemporary Communism* (Belmont, Calif.: Wadsworth, 1963), pp. 88-92.

71. Guenther Roth, "Personal Relationship, Patrimonialism and Empire Building in the New States," *World Politics*, XX (January, 1968), pp. 198-99.

72. Most recently in F. A. Hayek, *Studies in Philosophy and Politics and Economics* (Chicago: University of Chicago Press, 1967).

73. Leon Smolinsky, "Planning without Theory 1917-67," *Survey*, LXIV (July, 1967), pp. 108-28.

74. Marshall Goldman, "Soviet Economic Growth Since the Revolution," *Current History*, LIII (October, 1967), pp. 230-35.

75. Karl-Eugen Wadekin, "Private Production in Soviet Agriculture," *Problems of Communism*, XVII (January-February, 1968), pp. 22-30.

76. Z. K. Brzezinski and S. P. Huntington, *Political Power: USA/USSR* (New York: Viking, 1964), pp. 9-14, 419-29.

77. Raymond Aron, *The Industrial Society* (New York: Frederick A. Praeger, 1967), p. 111.

78. Karl Deutsch, *The Nerves of Government* (New York: The Free Press, 1963), p. 162.

79. P. J. D. Wiles, "Fifty Years After: What Future for Communism," *Lloyds Bank Review*, LXXXVI (October, 1967), p. 39.

80. Waldemar Gurian, "Totalitarianism as Political Religion," in C. J. Friedrich (ed.), *Totalitarianism, op. cit.*, pp. 119-29.

81. Raymond Aron, *Democracy and Totalitarianism* (New York: Frederick A. Praeger, 1969). Originally published by Gallimard in 1965.

82. Walter Hirsch, "The Autonomy of Science in Totalitarian Societies," *Social Forces*, XL (October, 1961), pp. 18-22.

83. Ghita Ionescu, *The Politics of the European Communist States* (New York: Frederick A. Praeger, 1967).

84. Robert Koehl, "Feudal Aspects of National Socialism," *American Political Science Review*, LIV, No. 4 (1960), pp. 921-33.

85. Ernst Nolte, *Three Faces of Fascism* (New York: Holt, Rinehart & Winston, 1966), p. 370.

86. Rauschning, *op. cit.*, pp. 21-26.

87. Isaac Deutscher, *The Prophet Armed: Trotsky, 1879-1921* (New York: Oxford University Press, 1954), p. 318.

88. H. Gordon Skilling, "Soviet and Communist Politics: A Comparative Approach," *Journal of Politics*, XXII (May, 1960), pp. 300-13.

89. Alex Inkeles, "Models in the Analysis of Soviet Society," *Survey*, LX (July, 1966), pp. 3-17.

90. A. G. Meyer, *The Soviet Political System: An Interpretation* (New York: Random House, 1966), among other places.

91. Allen Kassof, "Administered Society: Totalitarianism Without Terror," *World Politics*, XVI (July, 1964), pp. 558-75.

92. Robert Tucker, "Toward a Comparative Politics of Movement-Regimes," *American Political Science Review*, LV, No. 2 (1961), pp. 281-93.

93. John Kautsky, *Communism and the Politics of Development* (New York: John Wiley & Sons, 1968), p. 162.

3.

The Evolving
Theory and Practice of
Totalitarian Regimes*

CARL J. FRIEDRICH

Like all major concepts of political discourse, totalitarianism has an ideological dimension. But this employment of a key concept, such as democracy, for purposes of political persuasion and propaganda need not prevent the political theorist or scientist from employing it, provided he is aware of such employment. The role of ideology is highly controversial in any case, and even though one may reject the notion that we have come to an "end of ideology,"[1] it is evident that the real effect of ideological motivation upon the actual policy-maker confronted with concrete situations is uncertain, to say the least. Except for those who worry about such ideological use, misuse, or

---

*The following study—prepared for the Annual Meeting of the American Political Science Association held in Chicago, Illinois, September 5-9, 1967—is an extension of the changed concept of totalitarianism involved in *Totalitarian Dictatorship and Autocracy* (cited as *TDA*), 1965. Since this work is readily available, only a few references will be made to it in the notes which follow, though the germane chapters provide much additional material and references.

abuse, it is now fairly generally agreed that the kinds of autocratic regimes that have sprung up in this century in the wake of movements of violent protest against existing political orders are different from past autocracies.

At the outset, these regimes were called "dictatorships," because of their seemingly temporary character. Stalin's rule, the first of these novel enterprises, pretended to be a continuation of the "dictatorship of the proletariat"; Mussolini's pretended to respond in a purely pragmatic way to an emergency. Hence the term is no longer quite appropriate.[2] They became totalitarian as the leadership perfected the instrumentalities of autocratic rule. The term totalitarian, deliberately and consciously employed by Mussolini, on the other hand, carries for many merely the implication that these dictatorships were particularly thorough and ruthless, and for others, specific notions related to their explicit ideologies and policies (these "essentialist" notions are discussed further below). In our view, an operational political science had best ascertain first how these regimes actually function by documented concrete observation and "define" this particular kind of autocracy by describing its operational parts. Totalitarianism in such empirical perspective is on the one hand the advocacy or justification of such a system of rule, on the other the syndrome of such a regime's outstanding traits in terms of their immanent rationale. In short, although both terms of reference are, like all political terms, surrounded by a haze of vaguer and conflicting notions, the term "totalitarian dictatorship" has been so widely used for designating these regimes that it seems the better part of wisdom to continue its employment if one wishes to communicate effectively about them. Such a statement does not, of course, settle the question of what are the distinguishing features of such regimes, apart from their being autocracies. They surely do not closely resemble the despotism of an Oriental potentate, or "the empire that was Rome." Nor can they be said to possess the *Gestalt* of a tyranny in a Greek *polis*, or the typical features of a hereditary absolute monarchy such as that of Louis XIV. All this is fairly obvious to any student of these historical models of autocracy when he even just glances at the regimes of Brezhnev and Kosygin, of Mao, or of Castro. Nor do the rulerships of Ho Chi Minh and Tito, to mention only two others, seem very similar to those of Frederick II of Prussia, Nero, Pisistratus, or Asoka. Considering themselves more perfect democracies than those operating in the West, it might be argued that this would be a suitable way to speak of these regimes, as I have done in discussions with Communists. It does not really matter as long as the distinguishing features of these regimes[3] are identified, preferably on the basis of their *own* documents.

Since it does not intrinsically matter whether a regime is called totalitarian or given some other adjectival designation, as long as the central features are identified and described with a reasonable degree of correspondence to the available documentation, *i.e.* reality, reviews of the divergent use or abuse of the term do not prove anything about the reality. They may be quite helpful in avoiding the pitfalls of a confusion which is purely verbal, but totalitarianism shares this difficulty with practically every other word in the vocabulary of politics. Even so seemingly definite a term as "war" has been shown to have been employed in approximately a hundred different senses;[4] and in order to cope with the range of definitional issues raised by the term "freedom," a leading American philosopher found himself obliged to organize a large team and produce a two-volume work.[5] Such reviews of the variations in meaning of key terms are the stock-in-trade of political studies and are always useful. But they do not prove that one or several of the referents to which the term in question refers do not exist, are not worthy of scientific study, or may not properly be referred to by the term in question, especially if no other more suitable term is suggested.

Now, it is my central contention that regimes have arisen in the twentieth century which, while patently autocracies and hence generically related to such other autocratic regimes as tyranny, despotic monarchy, absolute monarchy, and military dictatorship, are quite demonstrably different from these other and older forms of autocracy. How they are designated is a secondary question.

The features which distinguish these regimes from other and older autocracies as well as from heterocracies[6] are six in number. They are, to recall what is by now a fairly generally accepted set of facts: (1) a totalist ideology; (2) a single party committed to this ideology and usually led by one man, the dictator; (3) a fully developed secret police; and three kinds of monopoly or, more precisely, monopolistic control: namely that of (a) mass communications; (b) operational weapons; (c) all organizations, including economic ones, thus involving a centrally-planned economy. I have purposely stated these features a bit differently from the way they were presented by me in earlier work because, as will be seen in the sequel, in this way some of the evolving theory and practice of totalitarian dictatorship are reflected. We might add that these six features could, if greater simplicity is desired, be grouped into three: a totalist ideology, a party reinforced by a secret police, and monopoly control of the three major forms of interpersonal confrontation in an industrial mass society. Such monopoly control is not necessarily exercised by the party. This should be stressed at the outset in order to forestall a misunderstanding which has arisen in some of the critical commentaries in my earlier work. The important point is that such a monopolistic control is in the hands of whatever "elite" rules the particular society and thereby constitutes its regime.

Before we elaborate on these features, it seems desirable to deal with some general issues. One is the question as to whether there might not be other characteristic features common to all such regimes. Brzezinski, while retaining the syndrome of operational features, would add its end or *telos*. In contrasting it with other autocracies, he says:

> Totalitarianism is a system in which technologically advanced instruments of political power are wielded with restraint by a centralized leadership of an elite movement, for the purpose of effecting a total social revolution, including the conditioning of man, on the basis of certain arbitrary ideological assumptions proclaimed by the leadership, in an atmosphere of coerced unanimity of the entire population.

And he adds that "this definition goes beyond Friedrich's descriptive syndrome of discernible characteristics . . . and attempts to point also to its essence."[7] But it is doubtful whether such an essentialist or teleological theory will remain tenable as totalitarianism matures. Other forms of autocracy have also known alternation between revolutionizing and stabilizing periods (*e.g.*, Peter the Great versus other Czars, Richelieu versus Louis XIV, Caesar versus later emperors). Ultimately, totalitarian regimes will probably resemble other governments so far as their ends or objectives are concerned.

It is probably in line with this that Brzezinski in a more recent paper[8] does not speak of totalitarianism at all. Yet, this is quite unfortunate. For how is one to assess the transformation which he sketches in terms of an "institutionalization" of power—an evasive term, since surely power is, and has been for a long time, institutionalized in the Soviet Union along the lines of the totalitarian syndrome—if no point of departure is precisely denoted? Statements like "obviously, the implementation of such institutional reforms would eventually lead to a profound transformation of the Soviet system" are indeed not only obvious but tautological, but they fail to state and make explicit what is the nature of the transformation. Is it a process of democratization? Or of liberalization? There seems to be a curious evasiveness about Brzezinski's conclusion that "in the meantime, the progressive transformation of the bureaucratic Communist dictatorship into a more pluralistic and institutionalized political system— even though still a system of one-party rule—seems essential if its degeneration is to be averted." Is this a prediction of transformation or one of degeneration?

In his carefree way another author, Michel Garder, had no difficulty in taking a stand:[9] Of course it is a degeneration, indeed an "agony" which the Soviet Union's regime is facing. And although he seems dimly to recognize the distinctive features of a totalitarian regime, as just sketched above, he confuses the analysis by calling it a "theocracy" because he sees its power-holders in a familiar, albeit misleading, analogy as "high priests" of a doctrine. Theocracies, as Max Weber noted, more properly called hierocracies, are a relatively rare species of political order quite different in important respects from the totalitarian dictatorships of our time. A revolutionary overthrow of this system is impending, Garder thinks, but what does that mean when even the death of Stalin is called a revolution (Garder, p. 195), and the steady evolution of Soviet totalitarianism is thus overdramatized? As far as one can make out, this impending "revolution" would consist in the further crystallization of an opposition of technicians. All close observers of the Soviet scene—and indeed of other totalitarian scenes—have for years been interested in the growing strength of this element which massive industrialization produces, and a variety of analyses and predictions on this score fill the literature on Soviet totalitarianism. There can be no question that its emergence has significantly altered the Soviet regime. But when tested against a clear and precise model of totalitarian dictatorship (of which it forms an important part), this evolution does not so far suggest that the Soviet regime is either basically different or that it is degenerating. In fact, it seems to be doing rather uncomfortably well when compared with its nontotalitarian rivals. They have their problems, as do other regimes, some of which they even have in common with other regimes, such as bureaucratization, but these problems are continuing to be solved within the system rather than by its abandonment, as will be more fully documented below. There is a constant danger of making one of these adjustments the central feature of a new and hence untotalitarian regime.

This mistake is narrowly avoided by Alfred Meyer. He undertook to re-evaluate the Soviet Union in terms of its total bureaucratization,[10] making this its key characteristic. That large-scale bureaucratization is part of the pattern, there can be no doubt; and we therefore included it in the analysis of totalitarian dictatorship.[11] But there are considerable difficulties resulting from the fact that such bureaucratization is largely lacking in some totalitarian dictatorships, or may be associated with a measure of de-bureaucratization, as was the case in Germany. The interference emanating from the party apparatchiks suggests another complication discussed briefly below.

Among other critics of the operational model outlined above, several have insisted that expansionism is another characteristic trait. In many ways it is. The ideological basis of these regimes calls for universal dominion, and the foreign policy of the Soviet Union, Mao, Hitler, and Mussolini has certainly been definitely expansionist, and Castro is moving in their path. On the other hand, there are small regimes of this type, such as Tito's Yugoslavia, which, though otherwise exhibiting all the characteristic features of these regimes, do not display any marked expansionism. Moreover, if such a system became worldwide, as it well may, it would be losing its "nature" when it could no longer expand. Even so, expansionism, often spoken of as a general trait of all states, though mistakenly I think, is certainly a common feature of many totalitarian dictatorships. It is debatable whether the recent action in Czechoslovakia of the Soviet Union and its allies fall under this heading: the proclamation of a Socialist Commonwealth suggests a desire on the part of its rulers to avoid such an interpretation.[12]

Presumably the most striking change in the theory and practice of totalitarian regimes appears to be the development of a substantial consensus in the Soviet Union. To be sure, the existence of such a consensus is difficult to prove under the conditions prevailing in the Soviet Union, and in the many writings on the subject one does not find any really convincing evidence of the kind which enables one to measure even the growing consensus in the Common Market area.[13] Even so, what evidence we do have, of an impressionistic nature provided by encounters with Soviet scholars, writers, and officials, all points so uniformly to such a conclusion that we are justified in assuming a consensus to exist until convincing evidence to the contrary is offered.

It is in this connection worth noting that the Fascist regimes did enjoy such a consensus. Their ideology was built upon the rock foundation of rooted nationalism, elaborated in Mussolini's case along the lines of a neo-Hegelian glorification of the state, whereas in Hitler's it was elaborated into the vision of a racist *Volksgemeinschaft*. But these doctrines were for the party stalwarts; for the masses of the populace, the distinguishing characteristic was a raucous and aggressive nationalism. This nationalism has now reappeared in the Communist regimes, stimulated by World War II in the case of the Soviet Union, by their defensive position vis-à-vis the Soviet Union and Germany in the case of the smaller popular democracies of Poland, Czechoslovakia, and the rest. This development increases, rather than decreases, the comparability of all the totalitarian regimes.[14]

There is, however, a countertrend which complicates comparison of the Communist and Fascist regimes. For the development of such a broad consensus has not, of course, kept either the Soviet Union or Maoist China or any of the small Communist regimes from continuing to evolve. This patent fact impedes the comparability with the Fascist systems which ended after a relatively brief life and have not been re-established so far. For this means that the Fascist totalitarianism was arrested after about twelve years of development, hence at a relatively early stage if the life-span of the Soviet Union, or even of the regimes established after 1945, is considered. What has become clear in the course of these years—since the mid-1950's—is that the regimes of Stalin and Hitler, far from providing the typical model of a totalitarian dictatorship, were rather extreme aberrations comparable in this respect to the rule of Ivan the Terrible, Nero, or Shih Huang-ti.

In this connection, the development of totalitarian dictatorship in the 1950's and 1960's reminds one of a well-known fact: the autocratic regimes of the past, lasting over long periods, experienced notable ups and downs in the degree of violence employed for their maintenance. Periods of relative order and internal peace, such as that of the Antonine Emperors, alternated with periods of fierce oppression and abuse of power. Anyone who takes to hand a history of China, Egypt, or Russia, can multiply the illustrations. These historical records suggest that this alternation of intensification and relaxation of autocratic power is cyclical, though the adventitious change in rulers, due to blood descent legitimacy, disrupted the cycle from time to time. Extraneous events, such as plagues and foreign invasions, may also cause deviations from the natural cycle of a gradual increase in violence. But barring such interference, the cycle seems to go forward to an

extreme followed by an, at times, radical reversal, a return
to the original state, and a resumption of the cycle. These
cyclical patterns of the past are subject to many variations,
especially nowadays to those engendered by the development of industry and technology. Observing this reversal
after the fall of Stalin, a certain number of analysts have
been inclined to attribute the "thaw," as it was hopefully
called at the time, to a permanent alteration in the nature
of the regime.[15] The argument has usually taken the form
of asserting that large-scale modern industry requires a
managerial elite which exhibits the characteristics of a
bureaucracy as analyzed by Max Weber—that is to say, a
predominantly rational behavior increasingly expressed in
legal rules. That this argument possesses a certain cogency
is clear. It is important to remember, however, that the
Hitlerian dictatorship pushed the German bureaucracy in
the opposite direction. Detailed studies have been able to
show that ideologically motivated deviations from bureaucratic rationality became frequent.[16] The evidence from
Communist dictatorships suggests that, in spite of a certain
amount of rationalization, limits are set by the ideologically framed mentality of the party apparatchik. Not only
in China, but also in Czechoslovakia, Poland, and other
Communist regimes, the meta-rational conditioning effects
of the prevalent belief system are quite powerful (as they
are elsewhere).

The oscillation between tight and loose control in an
autocratic regime probably typically extends over many
years, and no quick conclusions ought to be drawn by the
scientific analyst from any such changes. More particularly, the appearance of additional legal rules and regula-
tions ought not to be mistaken for the ineluctable
harbingers of the advent of the rule of law.[17] Such
legalization may be nonetheless very important in shaping
the totalitarian model—as indeed it was in the European
absolute monarchies and in the Roman Empire. It may

well be that such a development would eventually lead to an abandonment of the totalitarian model. In this connection, Brzezinski and Huntington have argued against the prospect of a convergence of the Soviet and American systems,[18] and they have adduced impressive evidence in support of their thesis. The question remains, it seems to me, an open one. Autocracies in the past have often succeeded in developing large bureaucratic systems as a reinforcement of the basic pattern of rule. Eisenstadt has been able to show, in an impressive volume,[19] that these empires spawned "bureaucratic societies." Without attempting to summarize here the range of his findings, it is germane to our present purpose to recall that these empires were "institutionalized" under very particular conditions. The most important of these conditions were: (1) the tendency of rulers toward implementing autonomous political goals; and (2) the development of certain relatively limited levels of differentiation in all the major spheres of these societies. The process he has analyzed bears many striking resemblances to what is going on at present in the Soviet Union and elsewhere in totalitarian regimes. For the assessment of the future of totalitarian systems, it is important to be aware that only when the two conditions noted above were present did the process of effective institutionalization of such bureaucratic empires succeed. This probably holds true for totalitarian regimes.

The "thaw" and related phenomena have raised further doubts about those efforts which sought to make certain psychological features decisive in assessing totalitarianism. There are a number of versions of this view, but they all stress the regime's asserted goal of remolding and transforming the human beings under its control in the image of its ideology. Hence the "essence" of the regime is said to be its total control of the everyday life of its subjects (called "citizens") and, more particularly, of their

thoughts and attitudes, as well as their activities. That
totalitarian regimes make such efforts, there can be no
doubt; that they do not succeed, is almost as certain. "The
particular criterion of totalitarian rule is the creeping rape
[*sic*!] of man by the perversion of his thoughts and his
social life," a leading exponent of this view has written.
"Totalitarian rule," he adds, "is the claim transformed into
political action that the world and social life are change-
able without limit."[20] As compared with this "essence," it
is asserted that organization and method are criteria of
secondary importance. There can be no question that the
statements just cited do, to some extent, describe a
significant feature of totalitarian rule, especially in its early
phases and in so far as the more passive members of
society are concerned. It highlights one of the psychological concomitants of totalitarianism. But there are a
number of serious objections to this theory. The first is
purely pragmatic. While it may be the intent of the
totalitarians to achieve total control, they are certainly
somewhat disappointed. No such control is actually
achieved even within the ranks of their party membership,
let alone over the population at large. The specific
procedures adopted in the effort to establish such total
control, the "passion for unanimity" as we have called it,
are highly significant, have evolved over time, have varied
greatly at different stages, and have become of secondary
importance when consensus has developed. As such, they
are better analyzed under such headings as propaganda, the
terror, and so forth, than in the perspective of the
individuals affected. They have perhaps been carried
farthest by the Chinese Communists in their methods of
thought control and brainwashing. One wonders whether
we are not here confronted with a cultural differential,
however, since Confucianism (as does Platonism) contains
this inclination to establish total control over the life of
the mind.[21] Countervailing tendencies, such as Mao's

"hundred flowers" slogan, suggest that even in China a sense of the importance of a measure of intellectual independence has manifested itself from time to time. The reference to Confucianism and Platonism leads to the second objection, which is a comparative and historical one. Such ideologically motivated concern for the whole man, such an intent upon total control, has occurred in other regimes in the past, notably in "theocratic" systems such as the Puritans' and the Moslems'. It has also found expression in some of the most renowned philosophical systems, especially that of Plato who certainly in *The Republic, The Statesman,* and *The Laws* advocates total control in the interest of good order in the community. This in turn has led to the profound and unfortunate misunderstanding of Plato as a totalitarian;[22] he was in fact an authoritarian, favoring the autocracy of the wise. Similar is the misinterpretation of certain forms of political rule in classical antiquity as "totalitarian," on the ground that in Sparta, for instance, "the life and activity of the population are continuously subject to a close regimentation by that state."[23] Furthermore, if this view of totalitarianism were to be accepted, it would be necessary to describe the order of medieval (as well as other) monasteries as totalitarian; for it is certainly often characterized by such a scheme of total control of the life of its inmates. Finally, much "primitive" government would have to be called totalitarian because of its close control of all participants.[24] As contrasted with such a diffuse and confusing interpretation, what is really the specific difference, the innovation, of the totalitarian regimes is the organization and methods developed and employed with the aid of modern technical devices in an effort to exercise as much control as possible in the service of an ideologically motivated movement dedicated to the total reconstruction of an allegedly moribund mass society. Since the phenomena alluded to above do exist and possess the common characteristic described, it seems desirable to use another term; a searching scientific researcher into the Chinese techniques of brainwashing has proposed the term "totalism" and "totalist" for this purpose. It seems a very helpful conceptual advance.[25] We could, then, sum up this part of our discussion by saying that totalitarian dictatorship is a system of autocratic rule for realizing totalist intentions under modern technical and political conditions.[26] Since modern political conditions signify a general acceptance of democracy, a totalitarian dictatorship can also be described as a "perfect democracy" in the sense that the people, represented by the party, which in turn is represented by its leaders, exercise total and unrestrained power.[27] The declared intention of creating a "new man" is a part of this general syndrome.[28]

This issue leads directly into the heatedly discussed problem of the role of ideology. Ever since Raymond Aron proclaimed, and Daniel Bell elaborated upon, the "end of ideology" in the mid-1950's, a controversy has been raging over the extent to which ideology constitutes a major factor in the syndrome of traits of totalitarian rule. Hannah Arendt had already argued, in her well-known book,[29] that to the top layer of totalitarian movements "ideological clichés are mere devices to organize the masses, and they [the leaders] feel no compunction about changing them according to the needs of the circumstances if only the organizing principle is kept intact."[30] This view is to a certain extent confirmed by recent research on the followers of Hitler. Biographies of Himmler, Goering, and others have shown that these men were basically committed to a man—Hitler—rather than to any ideology.[31] But this way of putting the matter is misleading, for in that relatively immature system Hitler was the prophet, the source of all ideology, and therefore commitment to him meant commitment to his ideas. The same can be said regarding Mussolini. He, as a matter of fact, proclaimed himself hostile to all ideas, celebrating himself and his movement as pragmatic.[32] As far as Stalin was concerned, he had amply demonstrated his doctrinaire commitment to Marxism-Leninism, as *he* interpreted it, by his own writings and speeches.

Therefore, it proved not very difficult for several writers to marshal against Arendt a number of convincing arguments.[33] Leaving aside the underdeveloped nontotalitarian polities, many of which have witnessed an extraordinary expansion of ideological politics, it is evident that the pretense of even the totalitarians experiencing an "end of ideology" was a flagrant case of ethnocentricity; for surely the potency of ideology in Communist China provides the background not only for the conflict with the Soviet Union,[34] but also for the Cultural Revolution.[35] A functional concept of ideology enables one to see contemporary trends in proper perspective. Some of the most serious misunderstandings about ideology are due to the fact that ideology has been taken in a dogmatic, even doctrinaire sense and seen as a static entity. This way of looking at ideology is, to a certain extent, a heritage of the view of Marx and his followers who understood ideology essentially as the "myth" of a particular social and political order. Ideologies do, usually, contain myths. But while myths are rather stable, ideologies are highly dynamic entities. Despite the fact that certain values, interests, and beliefs may persist over long periods in specific ideologies, they are, as action-related systems of ideas, subject to constant change.[36]

It is therefore part of the influence of ideologies, and not an argument against it, that the rulers of totalitarian systems are engaged in transforming it. These reinterpretations are, on the contrary, proof of their deep-seated commitment. Mao may well, as Lowenthal has persuasively argued, have "stood the Marxian dialectic on its head again" by abandoning its materialist and proletarian class analysis;[37] however, it did not mean an abandonment, but a reinforcement of ideological rivalry. And so does the steady elaboration of Soviet ideology at the twentieth, twenty-first, and twenty-second party congresses. These changes illustrate the plasticity of Bolshevik ideology, and therefore its vitality, rather than its end.

Ideology is so vitally related to the political process in literate societies that, far from passing away, ideologies are likely to increase in importance. This proposition has in recent years been demonstrated by the way in which the conflict between the Soviet Union and Communist China—by no means only ideological, of course—has found expression in ideological terms. It was clearly manifest in *The Fundamentals of Marxism-Leninism* issued in the Soviet Union in 1959, and has since been reinforced by the new party program of the CPSU.[38] As one searching student of these matters, with whose basic position we incline to agree, has written, "One cannot stress too much that the partners to the Sino-Soviet alliance are dedicated to a common purpose and bound together by a common ideology." And he adds in a footnote that, of course, such an ideology divides as well as brings together its believers, but that there remains a common commitment. Statements such as these rest upon the proposition that "to the Communists, theory explains and orders reality at the same time as it *provides a program for action.*[39] Ideologies are, in short, action-related systems of ideas. If this activist aspect of ideology is neglected, if ideologies are equated with any belief system or syndrome of ideas, as is often done especially in sociological writings,[40] great confusion results. In any case, when we spoke of a totalist ideology as a feature of totalitarian rule, we meant to have ideology understood in this way.

Some of the contributions to an understanding of totalitarianism have exaggerated the role of ideology, making it in fact the basis of a genetic theory. Let it be said here in passing that no satisfactory general genetic theory which would truly explain *why* totalitarianism appeared in the twentieth century has been put forward. It is a mistake to believe that its builders advocated it, though Italian Fascist rhetoric tended to glory in it. These systems evolved in response to a series of crises which they confronted as the regime struggled to realize the action program its totalist ideology called for. In stating the matter thus, we imply the vital role which ideology plays in the genesis of a totalitarian regime. Hence the exploration of ideological issues remains an important part of the changing theory and practice of totalitarianism. A considerable contribution to an understanding of Fascist theory was made by Ernst Nolte, who undertook to relate Italian fascism and National Socialism to the ideology of the *Action Française* group.[41] It is a subtly argued study in intellectual history, but it overestimates both the role of ideology in fascism-nazism, and the general significance of the phenomenon. He claims that the epoch from 1919 to 1945 was so decisively molded by fascism that it must be considered the key characteristic of the era. Surely, in long range perspective, it is more nearly the Russian Revolution and its aftermath, of which fascism is one important element, which dominated that era. The author himself argues that "fascism is anti-Marxism" and that "almost identical and yet typically modified methods" relate these regimes. Nolte goes beyond these characterizations to a "second level." Here he sees the Fascists as engaged in a "life and death struggle of the sovereign, martial, inwardly antagonistic group." Beyond this level lies still another one which the author considers the most fundamental. This is the level of "resistance to transcendence." It is not possible, for lack of space, to trace the author's rather

turgid argument.[42] The key point, namely that Hitler was
not an "incomprehensible accident" but "was possessed by
'something' " which was neither casual nor trivial, namely
a hatred for the human in man, is probably sound. Thus
the victims of Hitler died "as the deputies in the most
desperate assault ever made upon the human being."

The issues which these statements raise form the heart
of another significant contribution, George L. Mosse's
study of the intellectual origins of the Third Reich.[43]
Written with much greater detachment and historical
perspective than such earlier works as Kolnay, McGovern,
and Viereck,[44] this work seeks to elucidate the ideas and
beliefs which fed the Hitlerian ideology. He identifies the
"flight from reality" as the common trait of Fascist
ideologies—"Fascists everywhere spurned existing social
and economic systems in favor of an irrational world
view . . . objectified in the form of a new religion"[45]—yet
insists that "we must not allow these similarities to
disguise the profound difference between German fascism
and the others of Western Europe." Very true—in the
historical perspective. It is an ever recurring argument, and
applies equally to the ideological dimension of communism in Russia, China, Poland, Yugoslavia, and so forth.
There is always the individual, the specific component
which must be taken into account, but this does not
gainsay the task of cogent generalization. When we are
concerned with totalitarian regimes, we are moving on this
rather abstract level. It is evident that only by discarding
the specific content of particular ideologies can the general
pattern of totalist ideologies be discerned. That is why the
term totalitarian has always been so obnoxious to the
sympathizers with one or another of these totalitarian
doctrines. Being themselves caught up in ideological
preoccupations, the substantive "meaning" of the particular struggle, they resent anyone who seeks to identify the
common features of all such struggles. If I may refer to a

very recent instance, it is quite striking how many of the characteristic elements of *Völkisch*, Fascist ideology reappear in such work as Frantz Fanon's writings on racism and colonialism.[46] Not only do we find the glorification of violence which is so striking a feature of totalitarianism in all its forms. Protesting against a Europe which has "murdered men everywhere" in the name of Man, he calls for something utterly vague which is, however, "different." There is talk of a "new history," of "going forward all the time, night and day," and finally, "comrades, we must turn over a new leaf, we must work out new concepts, and try to set afoot a new man." It is not without interest that Fanon agrees with Hannah Arendt about the "totalitarian character of colonial exploitation." What he does not see is the fact that much of the reaction to it is also totalitarian in nature.

The key issue here is, as just mentioned, that of the glorification of violence. It is intrinsic to Marx's doctrine of the class struggle; its implications were elaborated by George Sorel; and Lenin's analysis of the revolutionary situation culminated in a vigorous call for violence. All this is well known. It follows logically from the total destruction which a totalitarian ideology asks for, and is found in all major totalitarian writings. It has lately celebrated new triumphs in Red China, where the Cultural Revolution was adroitly launched for the very purpose of enlisting the enthusiasm of youth in a new reign of violence to revive the flagging revolutionary spirit.[47]

In an interesting essay on *The Face of Violence*, J. Bronowski has sought to elucidate this ubiquity of violence. "Violence is an impulse we all share," he wrote, and "the love of violence is . . . the ancient and symbolic gesture of man against the constraints of society." This is a

theme which Camus highlighted in *L'Homme Révolté*.[48]
It has recently been made part of a very interesting study
on the response of the literary man to the totalitarian
world. In the center of this study we find an analysis of
four German and Austrian writers: Franz Kafka, Robert
Musil, Hermann Broch, and Heimito von Doderer.[49] The
author more particularly calls attention to the close
relationship of the "anarchy of drives" to the world of
totalitarianism; that is to say, he interprets the "apocalyptic erotic novel" as the mirror of a general anomie.
"Sexualism and total state are . . . the result of a pathologi-
cal alienation from reality"—it is basically the same theme
that Nolte suggests when he speaks of "resistance to
transcendence," and Mosse when he depicts the "flight
from reality." Under the influence of various psychoana-
lytic theories such as Erich Fromm's *Escape from Freedom*, we are confronted here with psychological "explanations" of the totalitarian syndrome which a book such as
that of Fanon (a psychiatrist) makes explicit by even
including cases to demonstrate his argument. In all this
writing—and there is an increasing amount of it—violence is
rightly seen as an ingredient of totalitarian and revolutionary ideologizing. It is therefore curious that even among
sophisticated students of these matters, there is still no
general recognition of the fact that besides the destruc-
tion-reconstruction syndrome, with its utopian aspect, the
positive evaluation of violence is crucial.[50] In a way this is
natural since the steady increase in over-all consensus in
the Soviet Union makes it possible to decentralize violence, allowing it to take the form of community pressure
and local vengeance, such as is predominant in China.

When one reflects upon these perspectives in the
evolution of the theory and practice of totalitarian
dictatorship, one finds oneself also concerned over the
third feature of such regimes, namely the employment of
an elaborate secret police generating the terror which used

to preoccupy the students of Stalinist Russia and Hitlerian Germany. There can be little question that the significance of this aspect of the totalitarian syndrome was overestimated in the past, especially in the writings of Arendt who, in her major work, predicted that the secret police would displace the party as the key instrumentality of such a regime.[51] Even so, there is such challenging testimony as the exclamation of a high Russian intelligence officer in his private papers. After reciting some murderous decisions of Khrushchev, he writes: "Who believes that Khrushchev has abolished terror? I do not, and nobody else does in the USSR."[52] We have numerous travelers' accounts, especially of people knowing Russian, telling of incidents clearly demonstrating the fear in which people live. What happened to a few intellectuals daring to demonstrate against the Soviet occupation of Czechoslovakia dramatically illustrates the persistence of terror and, what is perhaps more important, the possibility of its reappearance at any moment when the rulers find it convenient. At the same time, it should be stressed that the conduct of government and politics in Maoist China and Castro's Cuba in the extent of mass employment of physical terror even exceeds what Stalin and Hitler did. For the extermination of the Jews[53] does not properly belong under this category: It had no function in the regime, as the terror techniques of a secret police have, but is the ideologically motivated consequence of what was, in effect, the liquidation of a minority placed beyond the pale of the community, the *Volksgemeinschaft.* [54]

A good deal more has been learned in recent years about the actual working of the terror systems of Hitler and Stalin. Both the by now well-known revelations of Khrushchev[55] and the Eichmann trial[56] have served to reveal new and revolting dimensions of these manipulations. Biographical studies of some of the key terrorists, notably Himmler, have added further to our knowledge.[57]

At the same time, it has been made clear by historical studies that terror and secret police cannot be taken by themselves as the decisive trait of totalitarian rule. In all autocracies, the secret police and its terror have played their role, and there is no need to review this material here. The distinguishing feature is here, as elsewhere, the mobilization of the scientific knowledge of an advanced technology, in the form of all kinds of machines for spying on people and sophisticated methods of psychic manipulation. Terror is at this point transformed into the more coercive forms of propaganda. Only in cooperation with the monopoly of mass communications can the secret police hope to accomplish its task: Terror and consensus become Siamese twins. There may be much freedom of expression, and even license, in such a regime, provided the sacred taboos of ideology and official policy are avoided, and provided such dissent is strictly individual and does not aspire to organized support.[58]

Another important qualification has arisen as a result of a more precise knowledge and better grasp of the practices of nontotalitarian regimes. The conduct during wartime apart, which assuredly resembles autocratic rule, elements of secret police operations turn up in constitutional democracies, and elements of the population may well be terrorized, especially racial minorities.[59] It is, therefore, necessary to be more specific in speaking of a secret police that is uncontrolled. From this viewpoint, the efforts at controlling it which have appeared in Yugoslavia, Poland, Czechoslovakia, and even in the Soviet Union, must be considered attempts to delimit and, at least in Yugoslavia, to eliminate totalitarianism. This was admittedly the thrust also in Czechoslovakia.[60]

Older and more stabilized totalitarian systems than the Mao and Castro regimes with their massive physical terror have been able to depend increasingly upon psychic terror.[61] This form of terror has, of course, always played a vital role: not only what actually went on in the Soviet concentration camps, but also what was believed to be going on was part of the terror. This aspect has again recently been portrayed with dramatic vividness by Alexander Solzhenitsyn in *The First Circle* (1968), but it is also a recurrent theme in the literature dealing with life in these regimes, such as Silone's *Bread and Wine*, Pasternak's *Dr. Zhivago*, or I. Litten's *Beyond Tears* and A. Seghers' *The Seventh Cross*. Such anxieties were sedulously cultivated by the wielders of this instrumentality of violence, and so were their other forms, *e.g.* the comrades' courts of the Khrushchev era. The psychological terror exercised by a group within a given society can, as a matter of fact, have a greater effect than the physical terror, and the mere existence of a secret police, quite apart from what it does, suffices to maintain this feature. It is closely related to the basic revolutionary thrust of these regimes. Where total change is intended, massive resistance is engendered; to break it, the adversaries of the regime have to be terrorized into submission. There develops the "passion for unanimity" already mentioned, which looks upon any sign of opposition, and even upon indifference, as a betrayal of the regime. The brutal, premeditated violence of the terror becomes thus rationally justified. Such totalitarian terror grows until it reaches the limit where it becomes self-defeating, as happened in the Soviet Union in the mid-1930's and again toward the end of Stalin's rule; it seems to have been reached in Maoist China. Indifference and apathy among the workers are clear signs of it. These may in part be overcome by a vigorous effort at increasing consensus, especially as the efforts at indoctrination through education bear fruit. On this score, obviously a regime which has lasted more than fifteen to twenty years has a distinct advantage.[62] Arendt has suggested that potential enemies are then substituted for real ones. This is true, but only up to a point, for often the "scapegoat" is a foreign power far removed from the everyday experience of the populace.

The rangy discussion about the role and practice of the terror under totalitarian rule affects, to some extent, the role of the party. It is by now generally conceded that Stalin's excessive terror practices were combined with a disregard of the party, and that the liquidation of this extreme form of secret police rule engendered a revival of the party's role under Stalin's successors.[63] Also, the importance of the party as the decisive factor in settling the problem of succession in such systems has become increasingly clear.[64] At the same time, it has become more widely recognized that the totalitarian party is different from its nontotalitarian counterpart; indeed, there exists a not inconsiderable group of scholars who would insist that these totalitarian organizations do not deserve the designation "party." But the prevailing view is that it is not only inconvenient to have to say "the so-called Communist party," but also there are actually significant features totalitarian and nontotalitarian parties have in common which justify the use of the word "party" as a generic term to designate a group of human beings which is stably organized with the objective of securing or maintaining for its leaders the control of the government, and with the further objective of giving its members, through such control, ideal and material benefits.[65] Surely, totalitarian parties possess these characteristics in common with other parties, as numerous recent studies have confirmed. But they are distinguished by autocratic leadership, which Lenin first proclaimed as essential; by exclusivity instead of free recruitment; and by the monopoly which they possess in exercising the typical party functions in the body politic.[66] Indeed, so central is their role that any autocratic regime which lacks such a party or has allowed it to wane, like Franco Spain, should not be considered a totalitarian regime. The role of these parties is, at the same time, the major objection to the suggestion of lumping totalitarian systems together with other one-party systems under the heading of movement-regimes.[67]

All these totalitarian parties have been confronted with the problem of bureaucratization of their cadres. Lenin, not yet engulfed in the totalitarian maelstrom, had, shortly before his death, very serious misgivings about the bureaucratic tendencies in the Bolshevik party—a situation that has often been commented upon by scholars and politicians, notably Trotsky. It also constituted a serious problem for Hitler. More recently, the spokesmen for so-called liberalization, especially for greater intellectual freedom and more room for initiative and enterprise in the economy, have sharply criticized the apparatchiks. One such critic has spoken recently of the "pseudosocialism of a terroristic bureaucracy" which is being "rehabilitated."[68] On the other hand, this trend toward bureaucratic stabilization has been hailed as heralding an abandonment of totalitarian dictatorship, as an increasingly complex economy requires the pragmatic, undogmatic approach of the managerial mind,[69] in spite of the fact that such total bureaucratization has been a hallmark of these regimes.[70] It may be noted in passing that, in contrast to the CPSU, we still do not have any searching, comprehensive, and scholarly study of the National Socialist Party (NSDAP)[71] although the various biographies and special studies, notably that by Reitlinger of the SS, have adumbrated various aspects of it.[72]

A certain confusion has arisen in recent years in connection with the discussion of opposition and dissent in totalitarian dictatorships. Some writers, having misinterpreted the stress on the monopoly of the party as "monolithic" in the sense of being without inner stresses and strains, have heralded the appearance of fissures as foreshadowing the end of totalitarian rule. Actually, and indeed inevitably if viewed in the perspective of the laws of politics, there have always been factions and dissent. Not only at the beginning, but throughout their history, factionalism has been a significant feature of Communist and Fascist parties, as of all parties. An interesting recent monograph has been devoted to factionalism in the Nazi party. [73] Ghita Ionescu's comparative study of the European Communist regimes has traced some of these developments in the broader perspective of their economic and social development.[74] H. Gordon Skilling has projected these developments in terms of his classification of oppositions as "factional," "fundamental," and "specific" opposition,[75] taking on the whole a less "optimistic view" of these developments and thereby staying closer to the *dénouement* of the summer of 1968;[76] he believes to be unanswerable the question as to "how far the process of opposition will develop and what effect it will have on the system as a whole." Wisely, he adds that "it is impossible to predict the degree to which the regimes will tolerate opposition."[77] All I would add is that once such a regime were to allow an institutionalized and public opposition, it would cease to be totalitarian, just as the forgoing of the mass communications monopoly, as envisaged in Czechoslovakia, would. The drama of that country's Communist regime's reform plans was precisely this potential for the evolution of a totalitarian party into a competitive one, eventually achieving something new, which its promoters called humanist socialism.[78]

As far as the three major monopolies, and more especially the organization monopoly and its corollary, centrally directed planning, are concerned, recent theory and practice have evolved steadily without causing any basic change of course. The far-flung debate in the Soviet Union over decentralization (technically of considerable significance),[79] the parallel development of a measure of "federal" devolution in Yugoslavia and Czechoslovakia, the breakdown of successive efforts at coping with the planning process in Maoist China and, more particularly, the utter failure of the "Great Leap Forward" of the communes (predicted by the Soviets out of their own experience)—these and other lesser practical experiences have precipitated some doubts. In the Soviet Union, the sharp questioning of established routines by men for whom Professor Lieberman is symptomatic continues. The exploration of possibilities for introducing a measure of competition into the centrally planned Soviet economy has led to a limited amount of loosening the tight controls. This trend has been discussed in the West under the heading of "liberalizing," though the liberalism does not appear to have reached even the degree of freedom practiced under the most absolute rulers in mercantilist Europe.[80] Whatever may turn out to be the merit of these changes, they by no means entail an abandonment of the ultimate monopoly of all decisional power by the top leadership. The same holds true for mass communications. This issue has been highlighted in recent years by intellectuals in the Soviet Union and other Communist regimes under the heading of censorship, and naturally so. Censorship is the instrumentality by which the monopoly of mass communications is maintained. Sakharov in his plea for intellectual freedom rightly insists that "the problem of censorship (in the broadest sense of the word) has been one of the central issues in the ideological struggle of the last few years." He adds that "we are all familiar with the passionate and closely argued appeal against censorship by the outstanding Soviet writer A. Solzhenitsyn," and he argues rightly that what holds for literature also holds for all other manifestations of social thought.[81] "The crippling censorship of Soviet artistic and political literature has again been intensified."[82] This same retrogression applies, of course, also to recent events in other Communist countries, more especially Czechoslovakia. It is very depressing to see censorship, and hence the control of all mass communications, revived in that unhappy country after the bold attempt to abandon it, and thereby see also the revival of totalitarian dictatorship.[83]

The literary value of some of the dissenting voices in Russia, Poland, and Yugoslavia is great and their appeal to the West justified, yet they rarely affect any wider public, and "only an extraordinary combination of circumstances could enable the writers and artists to launch a movement of actual resistance."[84]

Before we turn to the problems of resistance under totalitarian rule, we might add that probably the greatest obstacle to the employment of totalitarian methods in underdeveloped countries is the difficulty of effectuating the three monopolies characteristic of a totalitarian regime. The point here once again is that such a system is in a sense an autocracy employing the means of an advanced technology under conditions of democratic legitimation.[85] This seems to be the reason why it has proved no easier to establish a totalitarian regime in technologically underdeveloped countries than a constitutional democracy. The administrative and statistical tools for the effective operation of such a system are simply not available, nor is the personnel which could use them.[86]

It has been our conviction for many years that the operation of resistance is a crucial aspect of totalitarian regimes. As already mentioned, one hesitates to speak of it as "opposition" since that term has acquired an operational meaning which is absent in the case of most resistance to totalitarian rule.[87] But while there is not and cannot be, on account of the organization monopoly, any effective opposition to totalitarian rule, there is a good deal of resistance. In spite of the effort of the totalitarians to destroy all separate group autonomies, there remain in all these regimes some groups that manage to offer some resistance. The family, the churches, the universities and other centers of technical knowledge, the writers and artists, must, if they are to survive, resist the total demands of their rulers. This was most persuasively argued once more by Academician Andrei D. Sakharov when he recently asserted that "intellectual freedom is essential to human society." His assertion has justly been acclaimed.[88] We have spoken of these elements as islands—"islands of separateness" in the totalitarian sea. The events and developments of recent years have reinforced rather than raised doubts concerning the ongoing significance of these efforts, including a certain amount of symbolic protest by isolated individuals.[89] Indeed, so strong were these "islands" in Red China that Mao resolved to launch a major attack upon them with his Cultural Revolution—a process which in functional perspective appears to parallel the great purges in the Soviet Union in the mid-1930's.

The struggle of people to maintain a measure of independence and thereby to mount an operationally effective resistance to the regime has been going on in all totalitarian regimes. The Hungarian uprising and the overthrow of Sukarno and Nkrumah are perhaps the most dramatic of these events, although the latter two occurred at a time when the regime had not yet achieved totalitarian maturity and they therefore resemble the overthrow of Perón. But the continued resistance of church and university in most of these systems is probably more nearly characteristic of its basic pattern. Recent events in Maoist China have revealed that resistance, even though passive for the most part, was a major factor in the difficulties which led to Mao's resumption of leadership

and his unloosening of the Cultural Revolution.[90] It seems
an open question whether Lin Piao, in an effort to cope
with resistance in the armed forces, decided to mobilize
Mao, or whether Mao initiated the new developments with
the help of Lin Piao. In any case, it is quite clear that those
"experts" who insisted that the regime was now so
stabilized that it should be recognized were as far from the
mark as those Sovietologists who considered Khrushchev
firmly in the saddle in the months immediately preceding
his overthrow.[91]

In many ways the most revealing and well-documented
(instead of speculative) evidence concerning the operation
of a widespread resistance under totalitarianism has come
from Germany as careful researches have deepened and
widened our understanding, especially of the background
of the July 20, 1944 attempt to overthrow Hitler.[92] Again,
carefully researched biographies of some of the key
figures, and more especially the study by Fraenkel and
Manvell,[93] have added significant dimensions not only to
an understanding of the resistance, but also of the
totalitarian regime itself. General Ludwig Beck, Count von
Stauffenberg, Leuschner, and Gerstein have been studied,
and their background elucidated, as has the entire group in
Terence Prittie's *Germans against Hitler.*[94] Prittie rightly
emphasizes the danger of glorifying this resistance by
giving its participants heroic stature, while at the same
time using Hitler as an alibi for the entire catastrophy.
There *is* this danger, and yet the recent research does point
to the conclusion that Hitler's role was decisive, and that it
is inadmissible to assume that a totalitarian movement
would have succeeded in Germany without him. The same
holds true for Italy. The situation is rather different in the
Communist regimes. In spite of the very great role which
men like Stalin and Mao, Gomulka and Tito, have played
in developing the totalitarian syndrome, it seems more
arguable whether their role was decisive. How one resolves

this problem is to some extent beyond empirical research and turns upon one's belief concerning the genesis and process of revolution.

Not as a conclusion but as a final reflection, I should like to suggest that perhaps the most important change in the theory and practice of totalitarianism, in the conception we have of it as an ongoing process of government, is the realization that totalitarian dictatorship, like other political phenomena, is a relative rather than an absolute category.[95] Instead of worrying about an "ideal type," the comparison of a number of different regimes, all corresponding to the model as we sketched it, reveals that it is quite meaningful to speak of totalitarian features in terms of more or less, and that it is meaningful also to speak of totalitarian trends.[96] Such trends actually manifest themselves even in regimes which are definitely not totalitarian, such as de Gaulle's or some of the one-party systems in underdeveloped countries; indeed, they are not absent in constitutional democracies such as the United States.[97] There exists also something we might term "totalitarian remnants" in other countries, such as the Federal Republic of Germany. These are issues that lie beyond the immediate purpose of the present paper, but they are part of the changing conception of totalitarianism. Indeed, the difficulties and even crises which are besetting the established but imperfect constitutional democracies are themselves significant elements in the ongoing process of re-evaluation to which this paper tries to make a contribution.

The various changes and experiments suggest that there exists a certain balance in the totalitarian syndrome which, when upset, may lead to serious disturbances. If the party is allowed to deteriorate, the terroristic secret police may get the upper hand. If, on the other hand, this police is too much restricted, the party may be overwhelmed by various economic and other influences. These potential imbalances also suggest that it is questionable to soften the concept of totalitarianism either by including under it all kinds of one-party regimes or by merely stressing its monopolistic features as contrasted with its dynamic core, namely the party, its leadership, and its ideology.[98] It is quite apparent that totalitarian movements, once they have seized power and commenced to build a totalitarian system, find themselves seriously troubled by the more utopian aspects of their ideology, as well as by the consequences of trying to put some of them into effect. It is equally apparent that in its efforts to cope with these difficulties a totalitarian regime matures, and that in this maturation process serious maladjustments develop and threaten its stability. The Soviet Union, more than any other totalitarian regime, has so far proved capable of overcoming these stresses and strains. Its totalitarianism, a novel form of autocracy, appears to be a highly dynamic form of government which is still evolving. Socialist legality may have an important role to play in the ritualization of its ideology as well as in the routinization of its inspirational appeal. For an increasing recognition of law and legal restraints even in the sphere of government may provide a middle ground between violence and anarchy, comparable to the monarchical absolutist regimes of Europe's past.

NOTES

1. The debate, precipitated by Raymond Aron's *Opium des Intellectuels*, will be discussed more fully below.

2. This range of issues I explored in an article "Diktatur" in *Sowjetsystem und Demokratische Gesellschaft—eine vergleichende Enzyklopädie* (Freiburg: Verlag Herder, 1967), pp. 1239 ff. (Soon to be published in English.) There also, a selective bibliography.

3. When we speak of features here, we are referring in a general way to the components of a morphological (structural) and operational (functional) theory. For these distinctions, see my *Man and His Government* (cited hereafter as *MG*) (New York: McGraw-Hill, 1963), introduction, pp. 1 ff.

4. Fritz Grob, *The Relativity of War and Peace* (New Haven, Conn.: Yale University Press, 1949).

5. Mortimer Adler, *Research on Freedom*, Vol. I, 1954, and *The Idea of Freedom*, 2 vols. (New York: Doubleday, 1958, 1961).

6. As a dichotomic alternative to autocracy, I suggested this term, some years ago, since *autos* refers to the self, whereas *heteros* refers to the other, so that an autocrat is only responsible to himself (besides God), whereas the heterocrat is responsible to another, who therefore in a measure controls him.

7. Z. K. Brzezinski, *Ideology and Power in Soviet Politics*, Rev. ed. (New York: Frederick A. Praeger, 1967), chap. 1.

8. Z. K. Brzezinski, "The Soviet Political System: Transformation or Degeneration?" in *Problems of Communism*, XV, No. 1 (January-February, 1966), pp. 1 ff.

9. Michel Garder, *L'Agonie du régime en Russie soviétique*, 1965.

10. Alfred G. Meyer, *The Soviet Political System* (New York: Random House, 1966), chap. 22.

11. See C. J. Friedrich and Z. K. Brzezinski, *Totalitarian Dictatorship and Autocracy*, Rev. ed. by C. J. Friedrich (New York: Frederick A. Praeger, 1967), (cited hereafter as *TDA*), chap. 16. Franz Neumann, in his *Behemoth* (London: Victor Gollanez, 1942), as well as in his *The Democratic and the Authoritarian State* (Chicago: The Free Press of Glencoe, 1957), stressed the role of the bureaucracy. Its crucial role in the development of the modern state altogether was emphasized in my *Constitutional Government and Democracy*, 4th ed. (Waltham, Mass.: Blaisdell, 1968) (hereafter cited as *CGD*), especially chaps. 2-6 where it is called the core of the modern state. A worthwhile selection of writings on totalitarianism has recently been published by Paul T. Mason, *Totalitarianism—Temporary Madness or Permanent Danger?* (Boston: D. C. Heath, 1967), with a discriminating introduction.

12. Stress on expansionism is found, *e.g.*, in Hannah Arendt's *The Origins of Totalitarianism* (New York: Harcourt, Brace, 1951), where imperialism is made the very basis and origin of totalitarianism.

13. In a forthcoming book of mine, *Europe: An Emergent Nation?* these developments are analyzed. See also the five studies by my collaborators in

this research: *Politische Dimensionen der europäischen Gemeinschaftsbildung* (Opladen: Westdeutscher Verlag, 1968).

14. Ivo K. Feierabend, "Expansionist and Isolationist Tendencies of Totalitarian Political Systems: A Theoretical Note," *Journal of Politics*, XXIV (1962), 733-42, gives a good analysis of divergent theories. For more recent developments, cf. Adam Ulam, *Expansion and Coexistence—The History of Soviet Foreign Policy, 1917-67* (New York: Frederick A. Praeger, 1968), especially chap. 12.

15. Mention might be made here of Isaac Deutscher, *Russia in Transition* (London: Hamish Hamilton, 1957).

16. Elke Frank, "The Role of Bureaucracy in Transition," *The Journal of Politics*, XXVIII (1966), 725-53. Her forthcoming study of the German diplomatic service, enlarging upon Paul Seabury's *The Wilhelmstrasse: A Study of German Diplomats under the Nazi Regime* (Berkeley: University of California Press, 1954), is a very good source; but see also the new study of Goebbels by Helmut Heiber in his introduction to *The Early Goebbels Diaries* (New York: Frederick A. Praeger, 1962); and other recent writings on the German National Socialist regime which are cited *infra*, n. 31.

17. Harold J. Berman, *Justice in the U.S.S.R.—An Interpretation of Soviet Law*, Rev. ed. (Cambridge, Mass.: Harvard University Press, 1963); the same, *Soviet Criminal Law and Procedure—The RSFSR Codes* (Cambridge, Mass.: Harvard University Press, 1966); the same, "The Struggle of Soviet Jurists against a Return to Stalinist Terror," *Slavic Review*, XXII (1963), 341 ff.; and the same (with James W. Spindler), "Soviet Comrades' Courts," *Washington Law Review*, XXXVIII (1963), 842-910. Further, see the literature cited in the notes to chap. 10 of *TDA*.

18. Z. K. Brzezinski and S. P. Huntington, *Political Power: USA/USSR, Similarities and Contrasts—Convergence or Evolution* (New York: Viking, 1964), esp. the concluding chapter.

19. S. N. Eisenstadt, *The Political Systems of Empires—The Rise and Fall of Historical Bureaucratic Societies* (New York: The Free Press, 1962); see also my review in *The American Historical Review*, 1964.

20. H. Buchheim, *Totalitäre Herrschaft—Wesen und Merkmale* (Munich, 1962), pp. 14, 24. (Now also available in English under the title *Totalitarian Rule* (Middletown, Conn.: Wesleyan University Press, 1968).

21. Robert J. Lifton, *Thought Reform and the Psychology of Totalism: A Study of Brainwashing in China* (New York: W. W. Norton, 1961).

22. Karl R. Popper (*The Open Society and Its Enemies*, Vol. I, *The Age of Plato*, [Princeton, N.J.; Princeton University Press, 1945]) is perhaps the most outspoken of the Plato critics. For a review of the entire controversy see Thomas L. Thorsen (ed.), *Plato, Totalitarian or Democrat?* (Englewood Cliffs, N.J.: Prentice-Hall, 1963), but the alternative suggested in the title is unsatisfactory, especially in light of J. L. Talmon, *The Origins of Totalitarian Democracy*, (New York: Frederick A. Praeger, 1961), and his more recent, *The Unique and the Universal* (New York: George Braziller, 1965), where the learned author proclaims: "Totalitarianism is the companion and function of

the permanent war-readiness of the race in its struggle for power. It is at the same time the logical outcome of the idea of organic determinism" (p. 150). For support of these statements, he refers to Nolte (see *infra*, n. 41).

23. A striking example of this diluted use of the term is Kurt von Fritz, "Totalitarismus und Demokratie im alten Griechenland und Rom," *Antike und Abendland*, No. 3 (1948), pp. 47-74.

24. Lucy P. Mair, *Primitive Government* (New York: Penguin, 1962), in chapter 2 shows how this extensive control may well be combined with "minimal government." For more recent trends in political anthropology, see Marc J. Swartz, Victor W. Turner, and Arthur Tuden, *Political Anthropology* (Chicago: Aldine, 1966), esp. their introduction, which provides a general review of the writings of anthropologists in this field. See also my article "Some Thoughts on the Relation of Political Theory to Anthropology," *American Political Science Review*, LXII, No. 2 (1968), 536-45, and the literature discussed there.

25. R. J. Lifton, *op. cit.*, esp. pp. 417-72. Cf. also Edgar H. Schein and associates, *Coercive Persuasion: A Sociological Analysis of the Brainwashing of American Civilians by the Chinese Communists* (New York: W. W. Norton, 1961).

26. On the importance of technology, see *TDA*, pp. 24-25 and elsewhere.

27. For a recent orthodox Soviet statement, cf. Viktor M. Tchikvadze, *Gosudarstvo demokratia Zakonosti*, 1967.

28. Klaus Mehnert has pointed out that "the most appealing traits of the Russians—their naturalness and candor—have suffered most." He considers this transformation "a permanent one." Cf. *Soviet Man and His World* (New York: Frederick A. Praeger, 1962), p. 35.

29. H. Arendt, *op. cit.*, pp. 372 ff.

30. *Ibid.*, p. 373.

31. Roger Manvell and Heinrich Fraenkel, *Goering* (New York: Simon & Schuster, 1962); the same, *Doctor Goebbels—His Life and Death* (New York: Simon & Schuster, 1960); Helmut Heiber, *op. cit.*; and Joseph Wulf, *Martin Bormann—Hitlers Schatten* (Gütersloh, 1962). See also the over-all study of Joachim C. Fest, *Das Gesicht des dritten Reiches—Profile einer totalitären Herrschaft* (Munich, 1963).

32. Dante L. Germino, *The Italian Fascist Party in Power: A Study in Totalitarian Rule* (Minneapolis: University of Minnesota Press, 1959), pp. 133 ff. See also the special issue of the *Journal of Contemporary History*, I (1966), esp. the papers by Mosse, Lyttelton, and Hugh Seton-Watson. See also Nolte, *infra*, n. 41. The almost universal lack of comprehension of the nature of a totalitarian movement such as Hitler's has been ably portrayed by Brigitte Granzow, *A Mirror of Nazism—British Opinion and the Emergence of Hitler, 1929-1963*, (New York: International Publications Service, 1964), with an introduction by Bernard Crick; for the later fateful consequences, cf. Martin Gilbert and Richard Gott, *The Appeasers* (Boston: Houghton Mifflin, 1963).

33. See especially Jeanne Hersch, *Idéologie et Réalité—Essai d'orientation politique* (Paris, 1956); and Joseph LaPalombara, "Decline of Ideology: A

Dissent and an Interpretation," *American Political Science Review*, LX, No. 1 (1966), 5-16; and S. Martin Lipset, "Some Further Comment . . . ," *ibid.*, pp. 17-18. See also the "debate" between Daniel Bell, George Lichtheim, and myself in *The Slavic Review*, XXIV (1965), 591 ff. Before long, the *Annales de la Philosophie Politique* will publish the papers contributed to a conference on "Ideology and Politics," and among them a searching critique of the "end of ideology" position from a Marxist viewpoint by Adam Schaff, "La notion fonctionelle de l'idéologie."

34. Donald S. Zagoria, *The Sino-Soviet Conflict, 1956-1961* (New York: Atheneum, 1964), esp. the introduction and chap. 8, but ideology is crucial throughout; see also the striking analysis by Richard Lowenthal, *World Communism—The Disintegration of a Secular Faith* (London: Oxford University Press, 1964), esp. chap. 5; and the studies edited by Morton Halperin, *Sino-Soviet Relations and Arms Control* (Cambridge, Mass.: MIT Press, 1967), esp. the editor's introduction.

35. On the Chinese Cultural Revolution, see the series of articles published in *Problems of Communism* under the over-all title, "The New Revolution," esp. Harry Gelman, "Mao and the Permanent Purge," and Theodore Chen, "A Nation in Agony" (XV, No. 6, 1966); Richard D. Baum, "Ideology Redivivus," and Franz Michael, "The Struggle for Power" (XVI, No. 3, 1967). Mr. Baum in particular views the Cultural Revolution as a form of "ideological revivalism" precipitated by the corrosion of the revolutionary ideology.

36. Cf. *MG*, chap. 5, and the literature cited there.

37. Lowenthal, *op. cit.*, pp. 109 ff., commenting on Mao Tse-tung's "The Chinese Revolution and the Chinese Communist Party" and "On Democracy" in Mao's *Selected Works*, Vol. III, 1954. Lowenthal rightly acknowledges that this and related problems of Mao's interpretation of Marxism-Leninism were first developed by Benjamin Schwartz in his *Chinese Communism and the Rise of Mao* (New York: Harper & Bros., 1951). Cf. for a more recent over-all assessment Juergen Domes, *Politik und Herrschaft in Rotchina*, 1965.

38. *Osnovy Marksizma-Leninizma (The Fundamentals of Marxism-Lenin-ism)*, (Moscow: State Publishing House, 1959). For the 1961 party program see Herbert Ritvo (ed.), *The New Soviet Society* (New York: New Leader, 1962); and for a comparison with earlier programs, Jan F. Triska (ed.), *Soviet Communism: Programs and Rules* (San Francisco: Chandler Publishing, 1962).

39. D. Zagoria, *op. cit.*, pp. 8 and 225.

40. Talcott Parsons, *The Social System* (Chicago: The Free Press of Glencoe, 1951), p. 349; similarly and following him is Herbert Spiro, *Government by Constitution* (New York: Random House, 1959), p. 180.

41. Ernst Nolte, *Three Faces of Fascism: Action Française, Italian Fascism, National Socialism* (New York: Holt, Rinehart & Winston, 1966). (German original, 1963.)

42. Nolte, *op. cit.*, esp. pp. 430 ff. Cf. also my review of the foregoing in *Modern Language Journal*, September, 1966.

43. George L. Mosse, *The Crisis of German Ideology: Intellectual Origins of the Third Reich* (New York: Grosset & Dunlap, 1964). Note the thoughtful

discussion of this issue by Hajo Holborn, "Origins and Political Character of Nazi Ideology," *Political Science Quarterly*, LXXIX (1964), 542 ff.: "Hitler derived his ideology from few sources, all of them of a rather low type. Many German writers during the Nazi period endeavoured to relate Hitler to the great classic tradition of German philosophy—Leibniz, Kant, Fichte, and Hegel—or even linked him with Luther. . . . But all the evidence that we possess forbids this interpretation" (p. 554).

44. Aurel Kolnay, *The War against the West*, 1938; William M. McGovern, *From Luther to Hitler—A History of Fascist-Nazi Philosophy* (Boston: Houghton Mifflin, 1941); Peter Viereck, *Metapolitics: From the Romantics to Hitler* (New York: G. P. Putnam, 1941).

45. Mosse, *op. cit.*, pp. 312-13.

46. Frantz Fanon, *The Wretched of the Earth* (New York: Grove Press, 1965). (French original *Les Damnés de la terre*, 1961.)

47. There is a curious parallel between Mao's Cultural Revolution and Stalin's purges of the 1930's: They both fit Brzezinski's theory of the role and function of the purge as stated in his book, *The Permanent Purge: Politics in Soviet Totalitarianism* (Cambridge, Mass.: Harvard University Press, 1956), the main thesis of which seemed until then to be put into doubt by Chinese experience under Mao. Cf. our comment in *TDA*, pp. 186 ff.

48. Albert Camus, *L'Homme Révolté*, 1951; (*The Rebel* [New York: Alfred A. Knopf, 1954]). Cf. also Simone Weil, *Oppression et Liberté*, 1955.

49. Cf. Wolfgang Rothe, *Schriftsteller und Totalitäre Welt*, 1966, and esp. pp. 65 ff. He analyzes particularly Robert Musil, *Der Mann ohne Eigenschaften*, 1952; Franz Kafka, *Das Schloss*, 1926; Hermann Broch, *Die Versucher*, 1953; and Heimto von Doderer, *Die Dämonen*, 1956, and *Die Merowinger*, 1962.

50. Z. K. Brzezinski, *The Soviet Bloc—Unity and Conflict* (Cambridge, Mass.: Harvard University Press, 1960), p. 384; cf. also the same, *Ideology and Power*, *op. cit.*, esp. pp. 97 ff.

51. Arendt, *op. cit.*, p. 368 it is argued that because of the affinity between the leadership of secret conspiratorial societies and the secret police, they "eventually would concentrate all power in the hands of the secret police."

52. Oleg Penkovskiy, *The Penkovskiy Papers*, with an introduction and commentary by Frank Gibney (New York: Doubleday, 1965), p. 291. Men who have attended international conferences in which some intimacy prevailed can testify from personal observation that quite a few colleagues from totalitarian regimes exhibit the kind of excessive fear about any criticism of their own regime which manifests their being subject to secret police terror, even if no representative of these organizations is present; that they very often are is demonstrated with many concrete examples by Penkovskiy.

53. Gerald Reitlinger, *The Final Solution*, Rev. ed. (Cranbury, N.J.; A.S. Barnes, 1961). (German 4th ed., 1961.)

54. It is therefore quite possible to write an analysis of the party system of the Nazis, as I recently did in a chapter of the forthcoming volume on

one-party systems that Clement Moore and Sam Huntington are editing, without dwelling on the ideologically conditioned extermination of the Jews, just as many writers on the Soviet Union do not mention the extermination of a number of national groups, including the persecution of the Jews or the horror of the extermination of the Polish elite for which see the scholarly study by J. K. Zawodny, *Death in the Forest: The Story of the Katyn Forest Massacre* (South Bend, Ind.: University of Notre Dame Press, 1962). Cf. also Wolfgang Schäfer, *NSDAP—Entwicklung und Struktur der Staatspartei des Dritten Reichs,* 1956.

55. For the text of Khrushchev's speech, cf. *The Anti-Stalin Campaign and International Communism* (New York: Columbia University, Research Institute on Communist Affairs, 1965), pp. 1-89; for sound comment, cf. Fainsod, *op. cit., infra,* n. 80, pp. 167 ff.

56. Y. Rogat, *The Eichmann Trial and the Rule of Law* (Santa Barbara: Fund for the Republic, 1961); Hannah Arendt, *Eichmann in Jerusalem: A Report on the Banality of Evil* (New York: Viking, 1963) has aroused very sharp protests because of its anti-Zionist slant, but remains the most revealing study of this particular evidence on the workings of the terror. The recently published record of the great Stalin purges, with an introduction by Robert Ruckes provides other impressive evidence.

57. Cf. Roger Manvell and Heinrich Fraenkel, *Heinrich Himmler* (New York: G. P. Putnam, 1965).

58. For this see, for example, Harold Swayze, *Political Control of Literature in the USSR, 1946-1959* (Cambridge, Mass.: Harvard University Press, 1962), and the papers from *Problems of Communism*, edited by A. Brumberg, entitled *Russia under Khrushchev* (1961), pp. 341-42.

59. One does not have to accept the facts and analysis of David Wise and Thomas B. Ross in their much criticized *The Invisible Government* (New York: Random House, 1964), to be deeply troubled by the trend which they highlight.

60. The evolution of Yugoslav politics makes it increasingly doubtful that Yugoslavia can be considered a totalitarian regime, largely because of the extent of autonomy (pluralism) that is developing in various spheres. Cf. Ghita Ionescu, *The Politics of the European Communist States* (New York: Frederick A. Praeger, 1967), which is discussed below. As for Czechoslovakia, it is highly significant that one of their key Communist intellectuals, as reported in *The New York Times*, April 14, 1968, interpreted the changes proposed as moving from a totalitarian to a democratic society. Cf. for Yugoslavia, besides the reports in *Problems of Communism* and the discussion in Ghita Ionescu and Isabel de Madariaga, *Opposition* (London, 1968), pp. 158 ff., S. Jankovic, "Jugoslavien nach den Säuberungen des Juli 1966," *Osteuropäische Rundschau*, 1967. Ionescu wants to apply the term "totalitarian" only to the Stalin and Hitler regimes, and adds that "it is impossible to call contemporary Spain or Yugoslavia 'totalitarian' in the same way as Nazi Germany and Stalinist Russia." I agree, but why should one? Totalitarian rule has greatly developed since then, as we have tried to show, and Spain is not

totalitarian in terms of our model anyhow. He goes on to ask: "Can one say that the UAR, Pakistan, and Paraguay are 'totalitarian' like Albania, or East Germany, or China?" I should answer: certainly not, and add that the possibility of distinguishing them thus is precisely the value of the category.

61. Chinese terror has differed from Soviet terror, as has often been remarked upon, and has at times given rise to serious misinterpretations about the "tolerance" of Mao and his followers. Not to "liquidate" classes was an adaptation to Chinese conditions. For a balanced statement, cf. Lowenthal *op. cit.*, chap. 5; and Mao's view of the permanent revolution, for which cf. *supra*, n. 37.

62. Cf. Allen Kassof, *The Soviet Youth Program: Regimentation and Rebellion* (Cambridge, Mass.: Harvard University Press, 1965); Bereday, Brinkmann, *et al.* (eds.), *The Changing Soviet School* (Boston: Houghton Mifflin, 1960); Klaus Mehnert, *op. cit.*, chap. 9 *et passim.*

63. See Leonard Schapiro, *The Communist Party of the Soviet Union* (New York: Random House, 1960); and the material contained in R. L. Braham (ed.), *Soviet Politics and Government: A Reader* (New York: Alfred A. Knopf, 1965), Section IV; as well as Fainsod, *op. cit. (infra,* n. 80), chap. II, and Meyer, *op. cit.*, Pt. II.

64. Howard R. Swearer, *The Politics of Succession in the USSR* (Boston: Little, Brown, 1964); and *MG*, chap. 28, on the general problem of succession.

65. *CGD*, 4th ed. (1968), chap. 20; the distinctive features of the totalitarian party were suggested by Lenin in *What Is to Be Done?* (1902) as strict discipline, total obedience, and unquestioning acceptance of the ideology; no party has ever been able to achieve these, of course.

66. Cf. Schapiro, *op. cit.* as well as the other references *supra*, n. 63.

67. Robert C. Tucker, *The Soviet Political Mind* (New York: Frederick A. Praeger, 1963), chap. 1, esp. at p. 7.

68. *Sakharov (as cited infra* n. 81), p. 66. Cf. also the paper by A. Hegedus, "Marx's Analysis of Bureaucracy and the Socialist Reality," in the work cited *infra*, n. 70.

69. Peter Christian Ludz, *Parteielite im Wandel—Funktionsaufbau, Sozialstruktur und Ideologie der SED Führung—Eine empirisch-systematische Untersuchung*, 2d ed., 1968, is perhaps the most penetrating of these studies; it deals primarily with the GDR. For others cf. Ionescu, *op. cit.*, esp. pp. 95 ff.

70. *TDA*, chap. 18; Meyer, *op. cit.*, whose main theme it is, esp. chap. 22. Cf. also Radovan Richta, Ota Klein, and Jindrich Zeleny, "The Dynamics of Change: The Interaction between Leadership, the Economy, the Organizational Structure, and the Society," to be included in a forthcoming volume on *Leadership in the USSR and Eastern Europe*, R. B. Farrell, (ed.), which is based on papers read at a conference held at Northwestern University, November 8-10, 1968. Cf. also the unpublished papers read at the IPSA Round Table in Salzburg, September, 1968, esp. the paper by Alexander Ort, which deals with the program of reform. The tie-in of these issues with the problem of *planning* cannot be explored here. It was a major theme at Salzburg.

71. An interesting beginning has been made by Schäfer, *op. cit. (supra,* n. 54). See also the discussion of factionalism in Joseph Nyarkomay, *Charisma and Factionalism in the Nazi Party,* 1967.

72. G. Reitlinger, *The SS: Alibi of a Nation* (New York: Viking, 1957); cf. also n. 57, *infra.*

73. Nyarkomay, *op. cit.*

74. Ionescu, *op. cit.*

75. H. Gordon Skilling, "Background to the Study of Opposition in Communist Eastern Europe," *Government and Opposition,* III (1968), pp. 294 ff. and pp. 296-298. Cf. also his *The Governments of Communist Eastern Europe* (New York: T. Y. Crowell, 1966), esp. pp. 36 ff. and 91 ff.

76. Skilling, "Background...," *op. cit.,* p. 321. See also Melvin Croan's review of Ionescu's work in *Survey,* LXVII (1968), pp. 156 ff.

77. Skilling, "Background...," *op. cit.,* p. 323.

78. The roots of this outlook can be traced to the conflicts within the Communist party in the early days. See, Leonard Schapiro, *The Origin of the Communist Autocracy, Political Opposition in the Soviet State. First Phase, 1917-1922* (Cambridge, Mass.: Harvard University Press, 1955); and more recently, the study by Robert Vincent Daniels, *The Conscience of the Revolution—Communist Opposition in Soviet Russia* (Cambridge, Mass.: Harvard University Press, 1960). At p. 407, Daniels states that Stalin succeeded where the opposition failed because "he put himself on the side of all the pressures which were working in the bureaucratic and totalitarian direction, and made himself their personification." This shrewd remark serves as a welcome reminder once more that the Soviet Union was not at the outset a totalitarian regime, but developed into one under the tender care of Big Brother Stalin.

79. This subject was discussed several times in round tables of IPSA, notably at Oxford and Geneva; cf. Klaus von Beyme, *Der Föderalismus in der Soviet Union,* 1964. See for a general overview, Meyer, *op. cit.,* pp. 259 ff.

80. Fainsold, *How Russia Is Ruled,* Rev. ed. (Cambridge Mass.: Harvard University Press, 1963). Cf. also Alec Nove, *The Soviet Economy,* 2d rev. ed. (New York: Frederick A. Praeger, 1968), chap. 9; Eli F. Heckscher, *Mercantilism,* 2d ed. (New York: Barnes & Noble, 1955).

81. Cf. Andrei Sakharov, *Progress, Coexistence and Intellectual Freedom,* as translated and published by *The New York Times,* with an introduction, afterword, and notes by Harrison E. Salisbury, 1968, p. 62. Salisbury, in n. 24, points out that Solzhenitsyn's plea was submitted to the Presidium of the Soviet Writers on May 16, 1967; it claimed that the censorship was "illegal" and "unconstitutional."

82. *Loc. cit.,* p. 63, where Sakharov calls the treatment of Solzhenitsyn a "disgrace." He also protests against the Daniel-Sinyavsky trial as "compromising" the Communist system.

83. It is striking how the Soviets, upon their arrival in Prague, immediately sought to monopolize the radio as the most important mass communication channel; equally striking was the Czechoslovak effort to counteract this

monopoly by operating secretly originated broadcasts. Cf. the remarkable document put together by a group of Czechoslovak historians, *The Black Book* (New York: Frederick A. Praeger, 1969).

84. Gail M. Lapidus in *TDA*, chap. 25, pp. 328 ff.; Swayze, *op. cit.*; Mehnert, *op. cit.*, chap. 11. For the early period before the consummation of totalitarian rule, cf. Robert V. Daniels, *op. cit.*

85. Meyer, *op. cit.*, pp. 298 ff. and chap. 22, would stress "total bureaucratization" as we did in chap. 18 of *TDA*.

86. *MG*, chap. 35; and my "Some Reflections on Constitutionalism for Emergent Political Orders," H. Spiro (ed.), *Patterns of African Development* (Englewood Cliffs, N.J.: Prentice-Hall, 1967); as well as the forthcoming Brookings Institution volume on this issue with contributions by Joseph LaPalombara, Lucian Pye, Samuel Huntington, and others.

87. Robert A. Dahl (ed.), *Political Oppositions in Western Democracies* (New Haven, Conn.: Yale University Press, 1966), in his preface and chaps. 11-13. Also, the British journal *Government and Opposition*, imaginatively edited by Ghita Ionescu, is focusing attention on the great range of problems connected with political opposition.

88. First reported in *The New York Times* on July 22, 1968, less than a month before the invasion of Czechoslovakia by the Soviet army, it has now been published, *op. cit. (supra*, n. 81).

89. Cf. also the studies cited in ns. 74-78 *supra*. Ionescu has suggested the term "contestation" for some of these activities. Cf. *Government and Opposition*, II (1967), 240-50. His article in this special issue was entitled "Control and Contestation in Some One-Party Systems." This issue also contained a helpful article on Poland by J. J. Wiatr and Adam Przeworski entitled "Control without Opposition," pp. 227 ff. See also the Wiatr article of the previous year in the *Polish Sociological Bulletin*, 1966.

90. Cf. the works cited in n. 35 and n. 37, *supra*.

91. Besides the papers cited *supra*, n. 37, see L. La Dany, "Mao's China: The Decline of a Dynasty," *Foreign Affairs*, XLV (1967), 610 ff.

92. Hans Rothfels, *The German Opposition to Hitler* (Chicago: Regnery, 1962); Terence Prittie, *Germans against Hitler* (Boston: Little, Brown, 1964); Roger Manvell and Heinrich Fraenkel, *The July Plot* (London: Bodley Head, 1964). Cf. also the discriminating review of the two preceding books and other publications by Ernst-August Roloff, "Das Dritte Reich und seine Widersacher," *Politische Vierteljahresschrift*, VII (1966), 61. See the very able discussion in *Der Deutsche Widerstand gegen Hitler*, Schmitthenner and Buchheim, (eds.), 1966, by Hans Mommsen entitled "Gesellschaftsbild und Verfassungspläne des deutschen Widerstands," pp. 73-167. Mommsen shows that the outlook predominant among these resistance fighters was very varied, that they were neither reactionaries nor revolutionaries (except for the Communists) but rather were broadly representative.

93. R. Manvell and H. Fraenkel, *The July Plot, op. cit.*

94. T. Prittie, *op. cit.*; Gert Buchheit, *Ludwig Beck, ein preussischer General* (Munich, 1964); Helmut Franz, Kurt Gerstein, *Aussenseiter des*

Widerstandes der Kirche gegen Hitler (Zurich, 1964); Joachim Kramarz, *Claus Graf Stauffenberg . . . Das Leben eines Offiziers* (Frankfurt, 1965); J. G. Leithauser, *Wilhelm Leuschner Ein Leben für die Republik* (Köln, 1962). The limits of church resistance have been somewhat prejudiciously emphasized by G. Lewy, *The Catholic Church and Nazi Germany* (New York: McGraw-Hill, 1964), as they were dramatized by Rolf Hochhuth, *Der Stellvertreter*, 1963. (*The Deputy* [New York: Grove, 1964].)

95. Such a view underlies, it seems to me, the hesitation of, for example, Alfred Meyer, *op. cit.*, to employ the term, and the discussion by Robert T. Holt and John E. Turner of early forms in terms of "classical" totalitarianism as contrasted with what we can observe now (see the concluding chapter of Holt and Turner (eds.), *Soviet Union: Paradox and Change* [New York: Holt, Rinehart & Winston, 1962]).

96. A totalitarian trend may be said to exist whenever one or another of the features of the totalitarian syndrome appear. One of them, a monopoly of operationally effective weapons, seems to be fairly universally in the hands of modern governments. By weakening the institutional structure and the belief system of a pluralistic constitutional order, it paves the way for a totalitarian take-over, if conditions become "ripe."

97. See the general chapters by Clement H. Moore and Samuel P. Huntington in their forthcoming volume on one-party systems to appear this year. Some of the attempts to pin the label of totalitarian on features of American society, such as its corporations, are, however, quite misleading, stemming as they do from a confused and overgeneralized notion of what the adjective totalitarian denotes. For special references see the paper by Barber in this volume.

98. This tendency is found in Raymond Aron, *Démocratie et totalitarisme* (Paris, 1964) (New York: Frederick A. Praeger, 1969) although the author adopts in substance, as shown on pp. 287-88, our model as outlined above. Cf. the review article by Martin Jaenicke, "Monopolismus und Pluralismus im Kommunistichen Herrschaftssystem," *Zeitschrift für Politik* XIV, No. 2 (June, 1967), 150-61. For the evolution of the Soviet conception of dictatorship, see my article "Diktatur" referred to *supra*, n. 2.